.10-Minute
OBEDIENCE

10-Minute OBEDIENCE

How to Effectively Train Your Dog in
10 Minutes a Day

AMY DAHL

WILLOW CREEK PRESS®

Published by Willow Creek Press, Inc.
P.O. Box 147, Minocqua, Wisconsin 54548
For information on other Willow Creek Press titles, call 1-800-850-9453

Edited by Amy Kolberg

Printed in the United States of America

ACKNOWLEDGEMENTS

This book could not have been written without the support, encouragement, and discussions with a number of people. Foremost I want to thank my family, John, Ruth, and Charles, for their patience and help doing my chores as I wrote. I have also learned a great deal about dog training from John, and had many productive discussions with him on the subject. The book is much better thanks to John's critical reading of the manuscript, and I thank him for his time and careful attention.

Ruth took many of the pictures, while Ruth, Charles, and their dogs taught me a great deal about how people and dogs learn together. I also want to thank Stephanie Roberson-Thomas for her photography. Stephanie's understanding of composition and how to illustrate training concepts was a great asset. So was her patience and dedication.

I've learned from many friends and fellow trainers, but want to particularly thank Sue Alexander for many interesting and productive discussions. Sue guided me through my first clumsy attempts at clicker training and has contributed greatly to my understanding of behavior, aggression, and canine learning.

Sue's willingness to discuss differences instead of criticizing them has made our conversations especially valuable.

My thanks to Christina Maness, Jim Pedersen, Madeleine Burgoyne, Tracy Misero and Hope and Alan Thomas who allowed me to include pictures of their dogs. Thanks also to all of the dog owners who have come to me for training help, and in turn have helped me learn to talk to owners about dogs.

Thanks to Skip Huckaby for his insight and encouragement. Thanks to Eric and Ann Cartwright and Melanie Foster for decisions that they made.

This book would not have come to be without Tom Petrie and Willow Creek Press. They believed in this book and encouraged me to write it, and let's just say I never knew anyone could be so patient.

Thanks to those who will never read this—the dogs. Above all, thanks to my first dog, Shasta, who made me a dog trainer and taught me a heck of a lot about love and life. Thanks especially to the other dogs whose stories are told in the book, Smoky, Salty, and Laddie.

TABLE OF CONTENTS

INTRODUCTION

Congratulations! Most likely, you are reading this because you have, or are thinking about getting a dog. Dog ownership can be incredibly rich and rewarding, bringing warmth, companionship, responsibility, and opportunities to learn and grow.

In my experience working with dogs and owners, I've seen that dog owners who receive good support from their breeder, obedience instructor, vet, knowledgeable friends, etc. most often have well-adjusted dogs that are fully integrated into their lives. My goal in writing this book is to become part of your support system, helping you have a harmonious and full relationship with your dog. I intend to make what is known about training and behavior modification accessible, with a minimum of theory and technical detail; to provide guidance on puppy rearing to help you raise your dog to be a cooperative and good citizen; to frame training, and interpret behavior, in a way that's sympathetic to your dog.

Dogs are important in our culture, and as such they have their own mythology. Dogs are like Lassie and Rin-Tin-Tin: hero dogs, wise dogs. Dogs are loyal. Dogs protect their owners. Dogs know things we don't know. Dogs know everything we think without being told. Dogs understand the subtleties of our culture in detail. More recently, we've learned that dogs are little (or not-so-little) wolves that have come to live in our homes, who must be kept firmly in place or they will challenge our authority and take over the house.

It is really not fair to apply all of these expectations to your dog. He is just one dog, after all. He starts out as a puppy, only a few weeks old, and what he knows are the things you give him the opportunity to learn. You can teach him to be a responsible, good citizen; by being fair, you can teach him to trust you; and by including him in your life, you can teach him to fit in with your routines and activities. But if he doesn't get everything right the first time, please give him the benefit of the doubt. Don't assume he knows what you expect. Instead, develop a plan to teach him what you want him to know.

Be skeptical of ideas about dogs that lead to adversarial interpretations and confrontational procedures. Confrontation rarely, if ever, improves anything in a relationship with a dog. Some of the interpretations of dog behavior today lead owners to paranoia about their dogs—fears of what might happen if they fail to "keep the dog in his place." This is regrettable.

When I got my first dog, a wise friend of mine told me, "trust the dog."

I had no experience with dogs, but had done a lot of reading. The words sank in and I tried to make sense of them. I couldn't. Finally I asked, "trust him to do what?" (I knew, at this point, what dog I was getting, and he was a he.)

My friend answered, "Trust the dog to be a dog."

I tried, and got maybe a little inkling of a sense of what this meant. But not much. I had a lot of respect for the person who said this, so I decided to "file it" for future reference, to reexamine it along the way and see if I could understand it any better. If I remember right, my friend declined, with a hint of amusement, to explain any further.

Years later, having trained a lot of dogs, I know my friend's advice was exactly right. It has come to define my attitude as a trainer. My friend was also right not to try to spell it out, but I'm going to say a little about trusting dogs.

Dogs have moods, and sometimes they get confused or distracted. Furthermore, mistakes are part of the learning process. Don't see every imperfection as cause to panic or worry, or to doubt your dog. Good trainers know through experience that a wide variety of dogs all get there in the end.

Whatever may happen day-to-day, the broader truth is that your dog will respond according to his nature as a dog, and if you present lessons effectively, he will learn. He won't necessarily do things right the first day, or the third day, or the fifth day, but patience and repetition will prevail. Believe in his ability to respond and learn, and see it through.

An owner who trusts his or her dog knows that everything the dog does is a reasonable response to circumstances, given his nature as a dog and the things he has, or has not, learned in the past. (As my friend would say, "it's OK.") If you don't like what your dog has done, you can develop a plan to teach him to respond differently another time. You can get there.

My strengths as a trainer, which I will try to share in this book, are:

1. Getting there in the end, while letting the dog be a dog along the way;
2. Being dynamic enough, and making training interesting enough, to keep the dog paying attention and motivate him; and
3. Being a control freak "with an asterisk(*)."

The asterisk suggests there's more to the story. I don't try to control everything, but I exercise a lot of control in places where control is a benefit. Training a dog well takes a certain amount of compulsion to control things. Effective training is all about what you control. It's not about controlling your dog's every move; it's about controlling yourself, the lesson, and aspects of the environment to make it easy for your dog to learn, and to make sure that he learns the right things.

Control is related to trust. Have you ever noticed dog owners that keep their dogs tightly reined in on a short leash? Typically the dogs lunge and scrabble as their owners struggle to restrain them. Other owners always seem to be grabbing their dogs and forcing them to do things, while the dogs resist. These owners seem anxious to control their dogs, but the dogs are anything but under control. With dogs, when we physically vie for control, we lose control.

There are also owners whose dogs walk with them calmly on a slack leash, paying attention in case they are asked to sit, or to do something else. These owners look confident. They look as though they trust their dogs—and their dogs are under control.

The trick to having a well-behaved, controllable dog is to back off. Control the things your dog wants, and control the environment in which he learns, while giving him the latitude to learn, make mistakes, and "be a dog." Your dog will respond and learn to control himself, and pay attention to you in order to get the things he wants.

Why Train?
Why would you want to train your dog? You don't have to, of course; lots of owners don't. One reason is to get the kind of manageable dog I've just described. Training also builds communication. You and your dog develop a vocabulary of commands and an awareness of one another's wishes that enables you to communicate without commands in many situations. The mental challenge is enriching for your dog, and I hope, fun for you as well. Being well-behaved and controllable, your dog can be more fully integrated into the family and included in some of your activities.

There are many ways to train dogs. When I train, I adapt the program to the individual dog, drawing on several effective training methods. For the owner training his or her own dog,

I have long thought that the key to success is not so much the dog's personality, but the owner's comfort with the method. In the obedience section of this book I have tried to minimize elements that are common stumbling blocks and present an approach that I hope dog owners will find intuitive. The obedience course consists of a series of exercises. Beginning in a familiar setting free of distractions, you will induce your dog to do an approximation of the exercise, using a mixture of techniques—whatever works. To get your dog to come to you the first few times, for example, you will move away from him. To get him to "stay," you will use an intuitive gesture, while to get him to "sit," you will push him into position.

Using repetition and reward, mainly praise, you will polish your dog's approximation of the exercise bit by bit into the finished product, adding details such as improved position, quicker response, longer duration, and greater distance, working on one detail at a time. You will gradually remove the inducements that initially got your dog to do the exercise in favor of a verbal command.

When your dog is able to do several exercises well in your distraction-free environment, you can add another element of challenge in the form of distractions, things that tend to divert his attention. Practicing at a very simple level will help him to succeed, and learn to ignore the distractions and focus on you. As he becomes more accomplished, you will integrate training into everyday life by practicing exercises in places where you will want to use them, and by utilizing a variety of privileges as rewards.

This approach draws mainly on traditional training methods for the initial teaching of the exercises. The practice of gradually shaping up an exercise from an approximate beginning, accepting imperfections as the dog learns, is in keeping with modern, positive-reinforcement methods. It is important to emphasize praise for what your dog does right, and to avoid punishing him for lack of perfection, as punishment tends to discourage dogs from trying new things. While dogs are capable of learning from both good and bad consequences, they are not equal and opposite. "Rewarding the good" and "punishing the bad" are not interchangeable in training situations.

My hope is that the approach of inducing and then practicing exercises will be easy and accessible; that reliance on repetition and reward, as opposed to fault-finding and punishment, will make training harmonious; and that the suggestions for distractions and diversifying rewards will make for a natural transition to good obedience responses in everyday life.

A Few Thoughts on Dogs, Ownership and Training

We don't know what dogs think. Scientists are learning more and more about their capabilities, but we cannot know what is going on inside their heads. We do know something about how dogs react, though, because we can observe them. In trying to understand your dog, stay away from theories and complicated explanations. They may seem to have the cachet of "science," but they don't. Science accepts observation, not speculation, as an authoritative way to know the world. Base your decisions about your dog on observation and simple explanations, like "dogs do what works."

We do know from observation that dogs are social animals, with considerable ability to learn and conform to social rules. We know that dogs' learning is situation-specific; they don't generalize as readily as we do. They need help from us to understand that, for example, we want them to respond to the same commands outdoors that we do indoors. We know that dogs' perceptions can be very subtle, and they can pick up on signals we don't know we're sending, so they appear to read our minds. We know that personality and behavior vary widely among dog breeds, as do aptitudes and interest in training. We know that dogs learn by doing and repeating actions, not by punishment.

Habits are accustomed ways of doing things, and are a big part of a dog's behavior, as they are in people. If your dog's habits are what you want, great; if not, it may take extra time and creativity to teach and establish a different, new habit in place of an old one. When behavior has been committed to habit, it is comforting to do it, and distressing to be prevented from it, so have some sympathy for the challenge your dog faces when you are asking him to change. When your dog has established a good habit, he won't require constant reward, but continuing to acknowledge good behavior with praise is a good idea.

Dog owners sometimes get hung up on thinking, "my dog shouldn't need that," referring to a prompt or reminder to behave a certain way. This attitude frequently leads to punishing the dog, unfairly in my view. Maybe he "shouldn't" need it, but he does. More likely we, not knowing everything about the dog's point of view, are overlooking some challenge that is making it harder for the dog than we think it is.

Training is not really about whether your dog "obeys" you. Training is about attaching consequences to actions in a way that a dog can understand. Make desired behavior pay and unwanted behavior not pay. Keep it simple. Make your dog expect that you'll follow through on rules and commands. Along the way he will learn that you are in control.

Timing is important to successful training. Good communication depends on good timing. Your dog will associate consequences with what he is doing at the moment, not what he did a few seconds, or hours before.

Feedback is also essential. When your dog is making an effort, he needs to know frequently whether he's meeting your approval or not. Don't miss an opportunity to praise him for making eye contact when he is on a "stay." Praise him any time he improves his position while heeling. As you progress, be alert for opportunities to provide feedback. Motivation, attention, and comprehension depend on it.

Respect that some effort is required when your dog does any exercise, including the simplest, even when he makes mistakes. Acknowledge his effort by giving him your attention and mild praise if he seems to need it to stay motivated.

Short training sessions work better than long ones. Ten minutes is a good length for many dogs. Your dog will concentrate better when he's fresh. He will perform better, and remember what it feels like to do things right. I've found that dogs retain their lessons better when they don't do too much in one session. Both of you are likely to be more attentive and motivated with short training sessions.

Learn what your dog likes and put it to work for you. Does he love to chase a ball? Keep a ball in your pocket and throw it when he has done something especially significant in training, such as his best-ever performance on an exercise, holding a long (boring) stay, or resisting a tempting distraction. Does he like to race outside, or play with the dog next door? Before you let him do this, get him to do a couple of his obedience exercises. His favorite activity is a nice, strong reward, and he is also getting practice paying attention in an exciting situation.

Know what your dog doesn't like and make sure it doesn't work against you. You don't want to unintentionally punish him for doing as you asked. If he is playing and having a good time, don't call him, and then pack him up and take him home. Go get him instead.

If you take your dog out in public, or invite people into your home, you are likely to receive unsolicited advice. Frequently this is repetition of one of the popular "theories" about dogs. Free advice is suspect. If the person dispensing it hasn't taken the time to listen to your concerns, then it probably doesn't apply to you. People who have good advice to offer usually do not press it on you; they are more likely to wait for you to ask.

This book has four sections. The first is all about raising a puppy, including house-training, socialization, dealing with age-related behavior, and laying the foundations for good manners and training. The information on house-training, socialization, and establishing good habits applies to older dogs as well.

A course in obedience training follows. The approach I've described works on a wide variety of dogs, young and old, from the already well-behaved to the wild, unruly, and disrespectful. Each exercise in the sequence is a prerequisite for those that follow. Even if your dog already responds to several commands, I recommend starting at the beginning and teaching the exercises in order.

The third section covers manners. Manners include walking nicely on leash without pulling, keeping paws on the floor rather than jumping on people, and seeking attention politely rather than with obnoxious demands. Mannerly behavior is taught using non-confrontational methods; we recognize that there is something the dog wants, and show him the polite way to seek it.

The last section addresses behavior problems. It describes several proven strategies for changing unwanted behavior, with examples that include most of the issues that concern dog owners. In many places in this book I advise against attempting punishment, and the explanation is in this section. It covers the shortcomings of punishment, the reasons it is usually ineffective, and what it would take to use it effectively. Because aggression is poorly understood by dog owners in general, this section includes a summary of several common types of aggression. This is not intended to be a guide to solving aggression problems by yourself, but as background to let you know that many aggression issues can be resolved.

True stories of dogs I have trained accompany the four sections of the book. The story of Salty, who as a puppy showed unusual and worrisome age-related behavior, is included with the section on puppy raising. My first dog, Shasta, was accomplished in obedience, which proved useful on a number of occasions. Shasta's story is told in the obedience section. Smoky was a dog who taught me a lot about manners and how they are learned, so his story goes with the section on manners. Finally, Laddie, who made a complete turnaround after nearly being put to sleep for his behavior, has his story told in the problem solving section.

As you raise, train, and live with your dog, I encourage you to use care in selecting the ideas you will apply to your dog, and to remember that just because everyone seems to be repeating something, that doesn't mean it's good advice. Trust your dog. He is what he is. He responds authentically to circumstances as he finds them. Give him the benefit of the doubt; if you don't like something he does, recognize that he probably has a reason for doing it that is much more likely to be accidental learning than a desire to antagonize you. Instead of getting angry, work out a program to teach him what you'd rather he do. Control the right things—the things that lead to coherent lessons for your dog.

I hope you will find satisfaction in training and understanding your dog that goes beyond doing exercises and solving a problem or two. I hope your life with your dog will be long and rewarding, and that you find this book helpful.

NAVIGATING PUPPYHOOD

Puppies are cute and adorable, but can be hard to manage. They chew, get into things they shouldn't, and make messes. They require housebreaking, training in manners, and exposure to a variety of people and places, referred to as "socialization," in order to become pleasant companions as adults.

With an understanding that puppy behavior is developmentally normal and a plan, you can enjoy your puppy, confident that she will develop into a pleasant adult. I will outline a sound method of housebreaking, advise you on socializing your puppy, identify behavior your puppy will outgrow with little effort from you, and give you tips to gently gain control over future adult behavior. I will also suggest constructive and fun activities, including an obedience introduction tailored to puppy attitude and attention span.

The goals of this book are to help you manage and enjoy your dog. In order to fully enjoy your dog, you will have to recognize that your puppy is not a blank slate, but an individual, many of whose personality traits are genetically determined. Trying to force a dog to change her nature is frustrating; accepting her individuality, and identifying and molding those aspects of behavior that you can modify, is a worthy and fun challenge. Dogs vary, for example, in their activity level, their need for attention, their playfulness, their enthusiasm for unfamiliar people and dogs, their sensitivity to others, and their desire to learn new behavior. Through socialization, we can help an individual become as adaptable and confident as her genes allow. Through training, we can teach manners, a few commands, and solve specific behavior problems. We can use what we learn in training a dog to find activities that will be rewarding for that individual. We will not, however, make an aloof dog into a social butterfly or turn a working-bred dog into a couch potato. Put simply, nature and nurture play complementary roles in the development of an individual dog. Putting our efforts into those things we can change, while accepting the rest, is essential to enjoyment of our dogs.

House-training

Perhaps the most pressing project with a new puppy is house-training. I recommend using a dog crate in housebreaking your puppy. In brief, this method makes use of a puppy's natural tendency not to soil the place where she sleeps. When confined to a small area, a puppy will "hold it." Then when you take her out, she is primed to relieve herself. By taking her to the same place every time, and praising her when she urinates or defecates (pees or poops) there, you can quickly teach her to go in that one place.

Following that, she will not need to relieve herself again for some time. Depending on her age, breed, and disposition, she might be "safe" for ten minutes or for an hour or two. During this time she can be at large in the house with little risk she will develop the bad habit of soiling rugs, furniture, etc. Using this approach it is possible to house-train a puppy without any punishment—a big benefit as punishment is easily misunderstood and can lead to house-training problems.

A dog crate can be an excellent tool to help teach your puppy citizenship. Many instances of problem behavior arise from inattentiveness to a puppy or dog. When the owner's attention is elsewhere, the puppy tries various things to get attention. The most obnoxious actions are rewarded with the

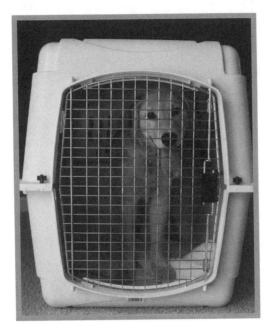

Puppy in crate.

owner's attention, and the puppy learns offensive behavior. By confining your puppy safely in a crate at times you must attend to something else, you can ensure that when she is out, you can concentrate on selectively rewarding her good behavior.

Most dogs seem to enjoy having a space that is their own, especially a small, enclosed space. Many owners keep a crate in the house when their dog grows up, sometimes removing the door, and find their dogs voluntarily spend time resting there.

One other benefit to familiarizing your puppy with a crate is that if the circumstances of her life require her to be confined to a crate at some point, the crate will be a source of security rather than of stress. She might need to spend time in a crate to recover from an injury or surgery, or in order to travel.

Choose a crate that has enough room for your puppy to stand up, turn around, and lie down, plus a little to allow for growth. The crate should not be so big that your puppy can curl up in one end with a big space at the other, as she may see a big space as a good toilet area.

These tips will make house-training easier, faster, and more pleasant for you and your puppy. For an adult dog, this same method works as well or better, because they have better bowel and bladder control than puppies.

One of the biggest challenges to crate training is a puppy's limited ability to "hold it" overnight. Getting up at night costs you sleep, may be an ordeal depending on the season and temperature, and may tempt you to cut corners such as letting her out the door instead of going out with her. Or you may be a heavy sleeper and fail to get up. The resulting mess is no fun to clean up and is not a training success. There are several things you can do to improve your puppy's nighttime control.

Feed her on a schedule, so that the last feeding is several hours before bedtime. Sometime after eating she will be thirsty, and drinking will stimulate both bowels and bladder. Take up her water a couple of hours before her last outing for the evening.

Feed your puppy a quality food. High-quality, nutrient-dense foods can be fed in smaller amounts, producing lower stool volumes and allowing your puppy greater control. If your puppy is expected to grow to be a large adult, you may choose to feed her a "large breed" puppy food. Although these diets are restricted in calories to promote slower growth, in my experience puppies eating them develop bowel control and crate train well as long as they are not overfed.

If your puppy's stools are loose, see your vet. Diarrhea in puppies is something to take seriously.

Be sure to go out with your puppy. If you just let her out the door, you won't know if she has relieved herself, or if she just wants to come in to get some attention. When you take her out, you can take her to the same spot each time, helping her learn what to do, and you will quickly see if she has any problems. You may need to walk her around for awhile before she "goes." Exercise patience! Give her minimal attention until she relieves herself. Then praise her.

If your puppy has been outside unsupervised, it is not safe to assume that she has relieved herself recently. More likely she has been loafing, and the stimulation of a change of scene plus attention from you will make her want to "go." Bringing her in for a play session is likely to lead to an accident and, I think, is one of the main reasons people struggle with housebreaking.

Many puppies make noise when they are first put in a crate. Usually they soon stop if left alone. If yours starts yammering after being quiet, she almost certainly needs to go outside. Take her out with no fanfare—say nothing—so she doesn't conclude that making noise gets her your attention.

For contrast, do give her attention and talk to her if she is quiet when you get her out. If it is nighttime, praise her when she relieves herself, but skip the free time in the house—put her right back in her crate.

Dogs show definite preferences as to where they relieve themselves, favoring absorbent surfaces. Be aware that carpets and rugs will seem like good places until you teach your puppy otherwise. "Safe" time on a rug will be less than on a rubber mat or a hard floor. Some puppies will be clean only in a crate containing no blankets or absorbent pads; others are fine with them.

Outdoors, most dogs would rather urinate on grass than on concrete or gravel. Many dogs prefer to defecate on dead leaves rather than grass. You might be able to shorten your waits outside with your puppy if you can identify places that suit her preferences.

"Accidents" in the house can be kept to a minimum with a good crate-training routine, but most puppies will have one or more. If you can interrupt your puppy in the early stage, get her attention using an excited, happy voice and quickly rush her outside to the place you want her to use. Calm down and wait there until she finishes, then praise her as usual. Clean up any mess inside as thoroughly as possible, as a lingering odor could cue her to use the indoor area again. A solution of vinegar in water (1 in 5), or a commercial enzymatic odor remover will help remove urine odor.

Some puppies urinate when they are excited, particularly when greeting someone and getting attention, or when they are intimidated or punished. Bending down over a puppy often triggers it. This "submissive urination" is thought to be involuntary. Punishment tends to make it worse. Almost all puppies outgrow this as they mature. Minimize damage by changing your routines, greeting your puppy outdoors, for example. Try not to call attention to episodes as you wait for your puppy to gain more physical and emotional self-control.

Very frequent urination can be a sign of a urinary tract infection and should be discussed with your vet.

Socialization

Puppies go through different developmental stages. Prior to about four months of age, they tend to approach new situations and experiences with relative confidence and lack of fear. Experiences that become familiar during this period, such as individual people and dogs, places, sights, sounds, car rides, crowds, and categories of people such as children, large men, people wearing hats, and culturally diverse people, will be met with confidence in later life. Dogs who get more exposure during this stage are better equipped to weather life's experiences without undue stress. Deliberately exposing a puppy to a variety of people, places, and experiences at this age is called socialization. The window of opportunity for puppy socialization lasts from the age at which puppies usually become available, around seven or eight weeks, up to about four months.

Time and effort spent socializing your puppy are an excellent investment. Poorly socialized dogs act threatened and stressed in unfamiliar situations. Fearful dogs may be aggressive, or may be severely stressed by experiences such as boarding, vet and groomer appointments, visitors to the house, or going on outings intended to be fun.

I have seen a number of dogs, adopted as adults, that would cringe and cower. Owners often take this as a sign their dog was abused. Lack of socialization can, however, result in such fearful behavior.

Give thought to your puppy's temperament and your life-style in deciding what experiences to emphasize. Will you travel and take her with you? Board her in a kennel or at the vet? Have lots of friends, business associates, or children's playmates over to your house? Plan experiences that will prepare her: take her for a short visit to the vet and have staff members give her attention and treats; have children you know to be gentle with dogs visit your home; walk her in places with lots of noise, hustle and bustle. Beginning with short car rides and making sure your puppy has fun at the destination will teach her to go in the car willingly and ride without stress, reducing the likelihood of carsickness.

Dog temperaments vary widely, some being more adaptable, others more cautious. Whatever your dog's nature, you can do a lot to reduce the stress she will experience as an adult, when exposed to new places and people, through proper socialization of the puppy. The more cautious she appears, the more you must attend to making sure her experiences are pleasant and never threatening. Keep new experiences brief, and help make them pleasant by equipping "strangers" with special treats ahead of time. You can give her treats yourself to help create favorable associations with a new setting.

It is a good idea to talk to your veterinarian about your plans to socialize your puppy. The best opportunities for socialization occur before the age of four months, when your puppy's vaccinations may not be completed, depending on your puppy's breed and your vet's protocols. Ask your vet about the local health risks, and what level of socialization outside the home he or she feels is safe. Balance health considerations with the need for socialization.

You may have bought your puppy for her protective value. If so, good socialization is all the more important. A dog can bark and intimidate strangers—and trained dogs are particularly intimidating, since it is clear they respond to their masters' orders—but the dog is more secure, and less likely to bite inappropriately, if she is well-socialized and not fearful.

Remedial socialization is still possible for those dogs that missed out prior to the age of four months. What if you have one of those dogs that will cringe and cower?

First, accept her. You will never make her totally other than what she is, so don't flood her with stressful situations in the hopes she'll straighten up. Instead, work to lessen her fears through counterconditioning (described in detail in the Problem Solving section). Identify things that she fears. Introduce them one at a time, at a low level that won't overwhelm her. If she fears strangers, for example, approach strangers only so close that she notices them, and no closer. Associate something good with the experience. Usually this means feeding her treats she really likes. After a short time, stop giving treats and move away from the stranger.

With a dog like this, you have to go slower, be more careful, and work harder to tip the balance to make experiences favorable than with a puppy. You can make a difference.

Normal, But Troublesome Puppy Behavior
Along with the cute playfulness, puppies do a few things that most of us don't like so well, including biting, growling, and chewing. Puppies do outgrow these developmentally normal behaviors, no matter what their owners do. There are, however, preferred ways to cope with them, which will lead to a better relationship.

It is normal for many puppies to bite playfully. When among their littermates, they show a range of aggressive behavior, growling fiercely as they attack. They learn to communicate so

Puppy biting another in play.

that play-aggression continues only as long as both are willing participants, and stops when one puppy has had enough.

When humans take a puppy home, they usually become her chief playmates, and that playful aggression manifests itself in biting hands and ankles, sometimes accompanied by fierce growling. While a puppy that has just been taken from its litter often nips gently, it is common for the biting to get harder and more painful as time goes by.

This is normal play—not an indication your puppy is trying to control you, or is destined to grow up to be aggressive. In fact your puppy will outgrow it eventually. Hard bites with sharp puppy teeth hurt, though! In addition, controlling the biting provides owners an excellent opportunity to develop communication with their puppies.

Puppies kept together nip gently because they get feedback from their littermates that lets them know when the bites get too painful. Being social animals, puppies are equipped to learn from feedback and adapt their behavior. We can imitate their communication to let our little biter know when enough is enough.

Puppies, when bitten too hard, give a high-pitched yipe and may withdraw from play. The offender learns that play stops at that level, and is careful to bite more softly next time. We can get the same reaction by giving a high-pitched "Ow!" and withdrawing attention for five to ten seconds. Sometimes a puppy will immediately bite again, but more softly—testing to find out what level is acceptable. Another "Ow!" will result in a still-gentler bite.

Learning bite inhibition: this puppy is eager to bite, but gentle.

Behaviorists describe this process as development of "bite inhibition," and believe that it leads to a safer adult dog. A bite-inhibited dog, they tell us, may close her mouth on human flesh under conditions of great surprise and distress, but will avoid biting down.

I have raised a lot of retriever puppies—some of the most aggressive play-biters—and most of them got the message very quickly with this treatment. A few puppies are more difficult, attacking with abandon, usually with plenty of noise, and if they notice attempts to stop them, respond even more fiercely.

This lack of responsiveness, fortunately, is temporary. Puppies can get worked up to a level of excitement where communication doesn't work well. Trying to control a puppy in this situation is a losing proposition. Better to stop interacting, thus ending the opportunity to practice bad behavior. There will be times when your puppy is more responsive. Barriers are useful. You can quickly stop out-of-control puppy aggression by stepping over a baby/puppy gate, or by putting a puppy in her crate. You can help her learn to calm herself by getting her out again after only a minute or two in the crate, rewarding her with attention if she is calm.

It is worth noting the circumstances when your puppy becomes so excited as to be out of control, so you can avoid them. Many puppies get carried away when people sit on the

Bending over to pet a puppy elicits calm, mannerly behavior.

floor, especially if they continue to pet and play with the puppy while she bites and growls, jumps up or rolls over. Holding a puppy or bending over to pet her, and petting her only when she is sitting or standing upright are less likely to get her so worked up.

Behavior that is not practiced does not become habit, including the behavior of getting emotionally out-of-control. If you or anyone in the family is inclined to think it's cute to get your puppy worked up, please stop and think about the consequences. A dog that habitually responds to people with emotional agitation, or *arousal,* will be difficult to control and possibly dangerous.

You are likely to hear of various ways to punish your puppy for biting. In my opinion, these methods only harm the relationship with a puppy. Owners miss out on the opportunity to develop communication and feedback. Punishment for normal puppy behavior can go wrong in a number of ways, inhibiting learning, teaching the puppy to fear her owner, or even triggering more biting, leading the owner to fear that the puppy is "aggressive" or "dominant."

It is also normal for puppies to investigate almost everything with their mouths. This can lead to chewing damage or, for those that swallow objects, life-threatening emergencies. The best strategy, in my opinion, is to prevent opportunities. Confine your puppy in a safe place when she cannot be supervised, and supervise her whenever she is not confined. By all means give her some safe, appropriate toys to chew and explore. Note that not all toys are safe for every dog! If you have a power chewer such as a Rottweiler or one of the retriever breeds, choose only toys designed for serious chewers, and inspect them regularly for damage, to prevent your puppy from swallowing broken-off pieces.

I am not a proponent of teaching and using the word, "no!" Most problem puppy behavior is developmentally normal and will go away on its own. All we need to do is prevent damage and keep the puppy safe. When supervising, we can stop unwanted behavior as it starts by distracting the puppy. There is no need to intimidate her. Calling her name, or saying anything in an exciting sing-song voice, clapping your hands, moving away and inviting her to chase, tossing a toy, or picking her up and carrying her into a different setting are all effective distractions.

Once in a while, an emergency may occur. Your puppy may try biting at an electrical cord, perhaps connected to a hot iron or a heavy lamp. A thunderous "NO!" will instantly distract almost all puppies, whether or not they have heard the word before. In general, the less shouting dogs hear, the more strongly they respond to it. (Routinely shouting at dogs is ineffectual; I think it just hardens an owner's feeling that his or her dog never listens.)

The confine-and-supervise approach gives owners the opportunity to interrupt any time their puppy begins doing something destructive or unwanted. The puppy is denied the opportunity to practice the unwanted behavior and, because of lack of exposure, it never becomes a habit.

Barking

Isolation for extended periods of time is not good for a puppy's development. If a puppy spends long periods of the day alone, she may develop a habit of barking. On the other hand, some puppies bark for attention in their crates even when given ample attention and interesting activities. The usual advice is to wait until the puppy is quiet before getting her out of the crate, selectively rewarding being quiet over being noisy. Some puppies bark so much, however, or bark any time their owner moves, that it seems impossible to catch them being quiet, and barking is rewarded.

Bark collars can help. Most of the trainers I know prefer the type that releases a spray of citronella whenever they detect a bark. The combination of spray and strong smell is an unpleasant consequence that discourages further barking. Use these collars when you can be present to supervise. Because they must be worn loosely in order to function properly, it is possible for a puppy to paw them off, chew and possibly swallow parts. In addition, when the citronella reservoir is empty, the puppy can bark without consequence, so supervision is needed to make sure it is kept full.

Used with supervision, in conjunction with adequate daily attention and stimulation, bark collars can help establish the habit of being quiet. They won't compensate for a lack of attention.

Remember that if your puppy begins barking after a period of quiet, she may need to go outside to relieve herself. Judgement is needed to balance housebreaking aims with the desire to control barking.

Growling

Some puppies are vocal. Owners are often concerned if they sometimes growl in response to attention. All the puppies I have known to do this grew up to be normal dogs, usually people-oriented dogs that loved attention. If you are concerned about your puppy's growling, I suggest you consult an experienced trainer or behaviorist who can help judge whether the growling is accompanied by body language indicating fear or aggression.

Never punish a dog for growling. If she feels threatened by something, punishment may increase her antipathy towards that object or person. Further, there is a danger that she will learn to remain silent when she feels threatened. Her fear is still there and she may feel a need to defend herself, but you and others will be unaware of it because of her silence. Far better that she let you know her feelings by growling than that she bite unpredictably.

Some dogs and puppies will growl possessively over food, toys, or other objects. Sometimes they act possessive of people or other dogs. This can be a concern as a puppy grows up. If the possessive behavior develops, the dog may become aggressive over her favored objects. This is called "resource guarding," and there are protocols for dealing with it, often with the help of an experienced trainer. Do not panic, however. In my experience, most puppies that are brought up to be secure and confident, and are taught obedience and manners, outgrow their possessive phase without professional help.

I am told that possessiveness is particularly common among the retrieving breeds, which is easy to believe as these dogs are focused on finding, getting, and possessing objects. I strongly recommend that every retriever puppy be taught to retrieve! Then, when she gets an object, her goal will be not to keep it, but to get someone to throw it for her.

Puppy Behavior and Adult Behavior

In raising a puppy, house-training and socializing her, we are looking forward, trying to prepare her to be a well-adjusted and pleasant adult. Give the project a boost by giving some thought to all of her behavior. Actions that are rewarded in a puppy will persist and become adult behavior. Maybe they're cute when your puppy does them, but do you want your full-sized dog to do the same?

My most important piece of advice is to avoid roughhousing with your puppy, now or later. Rough play with a dog invites her to treat people roughly, a habit she could carry into adulthood. It undermines your other efforts to teach manners and appropriate behavior. The mixed message is confusing and may make her insecure. Roughhousing has the potential to make a dog dangerous in three ways. First, she learns to be uninhibited about biting and jumping on people. Second, she learns to habitually respond to people in a state of agitation or "arousal," which is a risk factor for biting. Third, her insecurity makes her overly reactive. The existence of some well-adjusted dogs who appear to roughhouse with their families does not mean that it is safe to do with every dog.

Roughhousing includes wrestling with a dog, pushing her, and waving hands around as she tries to mouth or bite them. Interactions that tend to get a dog "worked up" should be avoided; reward your puppy with attention when she is calm. If she cannot calm herself, remove her from interaction with people for a short time so she can settle down.

You can pet your puppy, groom her, hold her, go for walks, and play games such as retrieving that don't involve directing her excitement at people.

Other common problems with adult dogs include jumping up to get attention, barking for attention, and even worse, tugging at your clothes for attention. Notice what these have in common: seeking attention. Attention is a powerful motivator for both puppies and adult dogs. Withholding attention, if you're consistent, can be effective at decreasing problem behavior. It works well on jumping (just ignore the jumping puppy, then bend down to pet her when she has all four paws on the floor), but has variable success with barking.

It's extremely easy to teach a dog annoying behaviors: just ignore her until she does something too annoying to ignore. My first dog, Shasta, loved to retrieve tennis balls. He would get one and toss it at me endlessly as I was trying to read or write. I would often sip a mug of coffee as I worked, and one day Shasta landed the dirty, spit-covered ball right in the mug, splashing coffee all over. Ugh. That got me to my feet. I don't remember whether I took the soggy ball outside to throw, or if I just cleaned up the mess and got more coffee. It was a win for Shasta, though. I could tell because from then on he aimed for the coffee, and became pretty adept at landing the ball in it.

More commonly dogs jump up, paw you, shove their heads into your lap, tug on your sleeve, or even bite in an effort to get attention. If being obnoxious gets your attention, your dog will learn to be obnoxious. This is yet another reason a dog crate is such an asset: you can keep your puppy out of trouble when your attention is elsewhere. Then when you have the time to concentrate on your puppy, you deliberately use attention as a reward for desired behavior. I will recommend some structured activities that help foster good behavior you can reward with attention.

Puppy energy and enthusiasm can lead them to respond to you by running up to you and crashing into your legs. Do not encourage this if you expect your puppy to be a big dog! At this age, withholding attention is usually enough to stop your puppy from making a habit of colliding with you. Dogs can also trip someone by going between their legs. You can prevent this from becoming a habit by standing with your feet together and making sure you don't ever pet your puppy and give her attention when she is standing between your legs.

Some activities are "self-reinforcing." They are inherently pleasurable to dogs, and the more a puppy does them, the more she will learn to want to do them. They are difficult to change once established. By far, the best approach is to prevent your puppy from doing them at all. Digging, foraging in the kitchen, and tipping over the trash can are all self-reinforcing. Don't let them start. Confine your puppy when you can't supervise her, and supervise her when she is not confined. Remember, punishment is not necessary; just make sure you are there to interrupt her when she starts scratching the ground, or sniffing at the trash cans.

Playing keep-away seems to have universal appeal among dogs. Many of them love to be chased, and they like to possess something and carry it in their mouths. Keep-away combines both of these. Avoid the mistake of inadvertently teaching your puppy to play keep-away with you! If she picks something up, ignore her or move away, getting her to follow you. Do not chase after her, especially if she has space in which to run.

Dashing past you out the door, and running off to tour the neighborhood are two more activities that can become bad habits. Again, prevention is the best strategy.

Some dogs, particularly females, want to lick a lot. I have found that while I can get them not to lick by withholding attention, they have seemed unhappy about it. Maybe for some dogs licking is an important part of a relationship. I've given in and let them lick me. For what it's worth, I don't think this is something we accidentally teach them. It seems to run in families and is probably part of a dog's inherent personality.

Recommended Activities

Structured activities provide opportunities for your puppy to have fun without constantly getting into the wrong things. They help establish a bond between you, building your importance in your puppy's eyes. They lay the foundation for future training, whether you teach formal obedience or just want to shape up your dog's manners a bit. And they help both of you develop confidence in one another.

Walking your dog is an excellent activity. If you have a safe open area, introduce off-lead walks first. Your puppy can learn to accompany you without having to adjust to a leash at the same time. Because you are not restricting her movement, she learns to keep track of you and stay with you. You can run away from her a short distance and get her to chase you, which is the foundation for coming when called. You can even hide and wait for her to find you. Keep this easy at first.

In preparation for walks on lead, give your puppy a chance to get used to a six-foot leash by attaching it to her collar and letting her drag it around for a short time. After a few sessions she will take in stride the momentary tugs when the leash catches on things.

Take her for a short on-leash walk in a place free of anything that might frighten her. Do your best to avoid pulling on the leash. If your puppy pulls, stand and let her, moving forward again after she stops. If she hangs back, keep the leash slack and try to encourage her forward by coaxing, body language, any means possible other than pulling. For most dogs, pulling

Any time your puppy pulls, stand still and wait for her to stop.

is learned. When they are pulled on, they respond by pulling, and quickly establish the habit.

Some active puppies can't seem to stay within six feet of their owners. You may have the best intentions not to pull on them, but they dance around at the end of the leash and the idea of moving closer to you doesn't occur to them. Frequently a longer "leash" will solve the problem, giving these gung-ho youngsters enough room that they can experience the good things that happen when they aren't pulling. Pet supply houses usually sell longe lines made for horse training, in lengths of 15 feet and more.

Picking up and holding your puppy is beneficial. Be sure to

On a longer line, your puppy experiences less pulling.

support her body so she is comfortable and secure. When your puppy relaxes while being held, you are in control and she is accepting your control and trusting you. If she struggles, be as gentle as you can while maintaining a firm and secure grip. Do not fight to make her relax; that will come in time as she learns you will not drop her or hurt her, and she can't get loose. If your puppy has been taught by her breeder to accept handling, she will happily lounge in your arms.

While holding your puppy, you can pet her and also control her head and mouth, if play-biting is a problem. Once she relaxes while you hold her, gently handle her paws, touch and

Holding a puppy teaches her to relax in response to attention.

lift her ears, touch her mouth and lift her lips to look at her teeth. Dogs can resist being touched in some of these places, and accustoming her to touch now will help with grooming and health care later on.

Introduce your puppy to grooming by brushing her gently with a soft brush. Touching and massaging her all over is also beneficial. Keep contact brief in any sensitive areas. With repetition they will become less sensitive. You can teach her to accept having her nails trimmed using treats—one per nail at first.

If you can get your puppy to chase and bite at a toy, I recommend teaching her to retrieve. Retrieving is a wonderful activity. It is fun for both of you, provides an easy way to exercise your dog, and teaches your puppy to willingly release objects

Puppy retrieving.

to humans. This prevents or reduces possessive behavior as well as stealing objects to play keep-away.

Many breeds of dogs will readily learn retrieving when they are puppies. Choose a visible, appealing object, such as a rolled up sock, a fuzzy paint roller, or a fleece toy. Hold it in front of your puppy's face or drag it along the ground to get her attention, then give it a short toss forward. If she grabs it praise her, call, and crouch down with your arms wide, to encourage her to come back.

If she doesn't come back, don't chase her. Wait for her to drop the object, get her attention and give her another toss, then quit. Getting her to chase it and pick it up is the most important part; coming back will come later.

Don't be in a rush to take the object. If your puppy comes back but wants to keep holding the toy, let her keep it for a few seconds while you make a fuss over her. Then gently open her mouth, and toss the object again while she is still eager to get it back. If you cannot gently pry her mouth open, try picking her up. This usually makes puppies drop what they are holding.

Very short sessions of two or three retrieves help to build a puppy's enthusiasm. If she starts to get bored she will lose interest or develop bad habits.

If you have been successful in getting your puppy to focus on an object, chase and pick it up, but she either runs away or lies down to chew on it, here are a few tricks that may get her back. First, try backing away or running away to get her to come toward you. You can also position yourself between your puppy and someplace she likes to be, or by a gate that leads back into the yard or her pen. If you are out with your car or truck, chances are she'd like to run under it, so throw away from the car so she needs to go past you to get back to it.

Another trick is to have two objects. When she gets one, get her attention and toss the other in the opposite direction so she has to run past you to get the other. You can pick up the first wherever she drops it. With repetition this game will get to look more and more like retrieving.

Introduction to Obedience
Puppies learn fast. Introducing obedience exercises between the ages of six weeks and six months can be fun and make training

easier down the road. Not only do they learn the exercises, the combination of puppy pliability with a gentle presentation of the exercises fosters cooperation.

Your goal in teaching obedience exercises to a puppy is "learning how to learn." Don't start requiring reliability or any standard of performance. You have more important fish to fry: developing communication and a good attitude toward future training. Trust in your puppy's potential, and do not get discouraged by daily or weekly ups and downs. Remember your puppy is developing fast, and may suddenly be intensely distracted by something she didn't even notice the day before. Don't misinterpret puppy development as willfulness or defiance! Just present the lessons, repeat, and wait and watch as your puppy responds.

Your Puppy's Name

Your puppy's name is, in effect, a command telling her to pay attention to you. You can help her learn her name quickly by saying it when circumstances lead her to pay attention to you. When she is at large and comes to you, say her name. When you are about to feed her, say her name. When you are about to pet and give her attention, say her name. Out for a walk, if you have been standing still, say her name as you begin to move.

Soon she will pay attention when she hears her name.

You weaken the association with her name or any other command if you use it at a time when your puppy will not respond appropriately. If she takes off after something more interesting, such as another puppy, and you repeatedly shout her name (or "here" or any other command), she practices ignoring you. That's something to avoid.

Any time a command isn't going to work—which will be the case when your puppy faces temptation greater than you've trained for—you're better off keeping your mouth shut.

Sit

There are many methods for teaching puppies to sit. I find placing them gently in position, using praise and repetition, works well.

Gently pushing a puppy into the "sit" position.

For this you can kneel on the floor, or set your puppy up on a bench or table. Place one hand on her chest, and the other on her rear end. Gently push back on the chest, and forward and down on the rear, and she should fold into a sitting position. Say "sit" as she does. Tell her "good girl!" and immediately release the pressure. If she gets up right away, fine. It gives you the opportunity to practice again.

I usually repeat this about 25 times in a session. This keeps the exercise from getting too long and boring (for both of you), but provides enough experience for the puppy to pick it up quickly. Before long she will begin sitting in response to a light touch, or as soon as she hears you say "sit." Continue to practice sitting as you work on more exercises, gently prompting your puppy if she is distracted and doesn't comply on her own.

Stay; Release Command

"Stay" follows easily from "sit." Most puppies become a little slower to get up after being placed in a sitting position many times. See if you can get your puppy up on her feet by patting her in the ribs with one hand and saying "OK!" This is your release command. It will let your puppy know, any time she has been concentrating for a period of time, that she can now relax and do as she likes. Some people use "free" on the grounds that they are less likely to say it accidentally or in conversation. Of course your release command can be any word you choose.

Now tell your puppy "sit" and then "stay," holding your hands ready but not touching her chest and rear. After about half a sec-

Introducing "stay".

ond, confirm for her that she's doing what you want by briefly holding her in the sitting position with both hands as you say calmly, "good." Then pat her in the ribs and say "OK!" as before.

Notice that you are teaching your puppy to continue what she is doing as you praise, waiting for the release command to break. There are times when it is useful to be able to let your dog know, by praise, that she is doing the right thing, without interrupting what she is doing. That is why I don't recommend using praise as your release.

Increase the time your puppy stays, bit by little bit. If she starts to "break," or get up before you give the "OK," catch her between your ready hands, press her back into the sitting position, and repeat "stay" as you remove the pressure. Finish the exercise promptly after a correction of this kind. She will learn faster if she gets it right the second time, and can compare the outcome with what happened when she got up too soon. By not asking her to stay too long, you improve the chances she will do it right without a mistake.

Once your puppy has a little experience with "stay," you can use feeding time for a little exercise in self-control. (For a really well-behaved dog, learn to use everything the dog likes to reward good behavior. Dogs seem to enjoy earning their benefits, thus acquiring some control over what happens to them.)

Now when it is time to feed your puppy, stand with the food bowl in your hand, say "sit," and watch for a response. With a puppy, I will usually set the food down at the first halfway pretense of a sit (say "OK"). At the next meal, expect a little better version, and so on, until your puppy is sitting neatly on command.

The next step is to get your puppy to remain in place as you lower the pan partway. Now that she has learned to "sit" in the face of the excitement of seeing and smelling her dinner, if she jumps up, you can raise the pan back up and remind her to "sit." Don't expect too much; a brief sit for a little movement of the bowl is a decent start. Say "OK" and set down the pan. By building, bit by bit, you can teach your puppy to contain herself as you reach down all the way to the floor, and then, to wait—as long as you like—for your "OK" release.

Down (Lie Down)

"Down" is a good command to teach your puppy, since sometimes adult dogs resist, and if they are strong, the resistance can be hard to overcome. As soon as your puppy is relaxing and accepting being placed in a sitting position, you can start placing her in a "down." Keeping one hand on her back, move the other under her chest behind her forelegs. While gently holding the back end down, gently lift your puppy's forelegs and chest forward, and lower them to the ground or table as you say "down." If she gets up on her own, say "OK!" If she just lies there, say "good," then give her a nice pat in the ribs as you give your release command.

Placing a puppy in a "down."

As with the "sit," do plenty of repetitions, and your puppy will start to lie down when she hears the command without needing to be placed. It is a good idea to continue practicing "sit," as otherwise puppies will start to lie down any time they are told to "sit."

Recall

"Recall" is the word trainers use for calling your dog to you, whether you use "here" as I do, or "come," or something else.

Trying to pull a puppy to you using a leash or long line may provoke resistance or even frighten her. Instead, take advantage of her natural behavior, saying her name and "here" (or "come") any time she heads towards you. If she is eager for food, giving her a treat or a few pieces of kibble will increase her motivation. You can also kneel down to pet her and lavish attention on her when she gets to you.

You can often induce a puppy to come running by kneeling down and spreading your arms wide as you call. Always use her name plus whatever recall command you choose.

Be careful to avoid calling her any time the consequences might be something she would try to avoid. This includes punishing her for anything, putting her in a crate, or otherwise putting an end to freedom and fun, whether she is playing with children or another dog—or digging holes and chewing up the landscaping. On the other hand, seize every opportunity to call her when you have something good in store, such as food, visitors, play opportunities, etc.

Crouching or kneeling with your arms wide invites a puppy to run to you.

As with her name, don't use the recall command when she is headed the other way and unlikely to listen, as that weakens the association between the command and the desired action of coming to you. If your puppy runs off, get control of her by whatever means you can, then go back to practicing.

Heel

"Heeling" means accompanying you at your side (the "heel position") as you walk, and coming to sit at your side when told. These are two different actions with the same command. Dogs are good at learning which to do depending on context, but need to be taught both actions. Coming to position can

Heel position.

confuse some dogs if walking is taught first. Thus with puppies I like to start with coming to position. Conventional heel position is on your left side, although some owners prefer their dogs to heel on the right.

Get your puppy's attention and see if you can get her to follow you as you move around. Once she is following you, try to get her to follow you in a counterclockwise circle. You face front the entire time, moving at first left and back, then right and finally forward. If your puppy is following you, she will make a circle, turning toward you when you move right and then facing front as you step forward. As she turns to face front, tell her "heel," then "sit," and finally "good!" Then pet her, give her a treat if you like, and tell her "OK!"

As your puppy learns this drill, say "heel" earlier and earlier in the sequence. Add a gesture, sweeping your left hand to your side and back. When you are giving the command and gesture as you begin to move, work on reducing the size of your circle while still getting her to come around to position. Bit by bit reduce the circle to a token step backward with your left foot, and then see if you can get your puppy to come around to heel using only the command and hand gesture. Praise enthusiastically if she does, release her immediately, and do something

Gesture and step backward to encourage your puppy to walk in a small circle and come to heel position.

else. When a dog makes a substantial step forward in training and is successful, it is better not to try to repeat it.

Now that your puppy has a good understanding of coming to heel position, you can readily use that to teach her to accompany you. Beginning with her sitting at your side, say "heel" as you move forward a couple of steps. If necessary, encourage her to "sit" when she catches up to you. Praise her or give her a treat. As she gets the idea, you can go a little farther between stops.

Do not expect a young puppy to "stay" or "heel" for more than a short time, however. Concentrating for an extended period of time without input requires focused attention, discipline, and effort to resist distraction. Puppies are capable of learning this level of discipline, but in my opinion, better long-term results are achieved by holding their attention for short spans, then encouraging them to exercise their curiosity.

Kennel
Whenever you put your puppy in her crate, say "kennel." Do the same when you want her to go in the car or any other enclosed space. At some point habit will take over, and she'll jump into anything if you point to it and say "kennel."

Expanding Your Puppy's Training
Obedience training becomes useful when it is expanded from the teaching setting and incorporated into daily life. You can lay an excellent groundwork for future reliability by identifying everyday experiences your puppy likes and using them as

training rewards. For example, when going for a walk, call your puppy and have her "sit" while you put on the leash. Before opening a door for her, have her sit and stay. Gradually teach her to stay while you open the door, as you did while setting down her food, until you release her with an "OK" or her name.

Make use of every activity your puppy enjoys. Does she have opportunities to play with other dogs? Get her to "sit" before you release her to play. When she can do that well, add another requirement, such as getting her to heel for a couple of seconds. No corrections are needed. If she doesn't pay attention to you, don't release her. She'll learn to concentrate on you and resist her impulses in order to get what she wants. Do help her be successful by adding requirements gradually.

Other people will often undermine your training efforts, with comments such as, "she's not hurting anything." If you really want to teach your puppy good manners, you will only let her interact with people who you know will reinforce good behavior, such as keeping her paws on the ground. Even if you choose not to go that far, and let her greet strangers, be sure to refrain from giving her any commands while others are paying attention to her. Their attention will reward her for disregarding your commands.

Throughout obedience work with your puppy, try not to take it personally when she is inattentive. Puppies go through various phases and can suddenly seem independent after having hung on your every word. Keep in mind that new things are always vying for their attention. One day they might discover that it feels TERRIFIC to stretch their legs and run; another they might be preoccupied with the newfound ability to follow a scent to its source. At any time a puppy may be distracted by something she never noticed before. Make allowances for your puppy's lack of maturity. If needed, in an exciting environment, you can revisit some of the cues you used to teach the exercises, such as a push on the rear as a reminder to "sit."

Conclusion

There's a lot to raising a puppy. We've covered the basics of housebreaking, socialization, dealing with age-specific behavior, laying the foundation for good adult behavior, recommended activities, and puppy obedience. We've emphasized the value of a dog crate in teaching specifics, such as housetraining, as well as promoting good behavior in general.

Much of the challenge of puppyhood is deciding what puppy behavior needs attention, and what can be accepted. I've described some age-specific behavior that goes away on its own, and encouraged you to evaluate other activities in terms of whether they're habits you want your puppy to have when she grows up. Try not to worry about puppy behavior. If you overlook something, you can always work on it later. And don't stake your happiness on day-to-day progress. Enjoy breakthroughs when they come, and accept mistakes and backsliding as part of learning.

Remember that puppies are individuals. Accept yours, and celebrate her individual personality while steering her gently in the direction of responsiveness and good adult habits. If your puppy's behavior seems outrageous, try to figure out if it's learned behavior or if it's an individual quirk. If it's learned, something in the puppy's environment is supporting it, and you can change that. If it's a quirk, extreme though it may seem, most likely your puppy will simply outgrow it, like Salty in the story. The exception would be fearfulness; if your puppy acts fearful, I suggest beginning right away to work on lessening her fears.

Remember to enjoy your puppy. Trust her to be a puppy, and to respond to the world around her with curiosity, an open mind, and good will; but also with impulsivity, a short attention span, and a canine set of perceptions. Don't forget to take pictures. Puppyhood is short; all too soon it will be just a memory.

SALTY

Salty was a singleton, the only puppy in his litter, a litter of one. He was delivered by C-section. The surgical team cleaned Salty up and put him in a box so they could attend to his mother. Salty climbed out. Someone grabbed him before he bailed off of the table. They put him in a bigger box and detailed someone to watch him. Salty was huge at one and a quarter pounds, incredibly cute, and the strongest newborn puppy anyone on my vet's staff had ever seen.

Candy, Salty's mother, was attentive, patient, and had lots of milk. Salty got all that milk for himself, and grew fast. By the time we separated them around eight weeks, it was almost impossible to believe he had come out of her. She was small for a Chesapeake Bay Retriever, and he was enormous.

Dog trainers worry some about singleton puppies. Competition, getting climbed over and shoved aside in the quest for milk, and later, social interaction with littermates, are important features of development for most puppies. Singletons miss out on all of that. I thought seriously about offering to have Candy wet-nurse some puppies from a litter of 10 whelped by C-section the same day, but couldn't be sure she wouldn't reject them. As a substitute I held, handled, and stimulated Salty every day.

Salty continued to be adorable as he grew, but he was independent. He didn't respond much to being held, and if I took him outside I would end up having to catch him. Fortunately, he would, sooner or later, find something of interest and stop to check it out. He never showed a tendency to follow me or to keep track of me, much less come back to me after his adventures.

Salty was eager to chase after a thrown paint roller and pick it up, then run off with it. We retriever trainers call that a "retrieve" even though it's missing the come-back-and-deliver part. We figure we can train any dog to come back and deliver, but we can't make them want to chase something and pick it up. So, although he was independent, Salty was a promising "retriever."

Salty was the most independent puppy I've ever worked with. I've raised other independent puppies. It was a lot of work, constantly trying to be the source of everything good in the puppy's life for minimal reward, as he or she largely ignored me. In every previous case, it turned out well in the end. The puppies grew up to be normally affectionate and trainable. But I wasn't sure about Salty. And that was before I began to notice his aggression.

I've had a number of people approach me for help because their puppies were showing extreme or worrisome behavior. Sometimes the puppies were very independent, one never wanted to be touched, and quite a few have been unusually vigorous about play-biting, and difficult to deter. I encouraged the owners to focus on following good puppy raising practices, as I did with my previous independent puppies, rather than reacting to the problems directly. In every case, the troubling behavior disappeared as the puppy matured. Salty's behavior was so far from normal, however, I wasn't at all confident it was something he was going to outgrow.

At the age of three months, Salty was strutting around as though he was a mature male and ruler of all he surveyed. That's a description of his posture; who knows what was going on in his mind. He would growl, snarl, and snap if I touched him or his feed pan while he was eating. Guarding behavior is common in Chesapeakes, but I haven't seen it to that degree at that age before or since. Salty was the most aggressive play-biter I ever worked with, and he started snarling, snapping, and biting me when I petted him.

I've known puppies to get snarly and bite when they are worked up into a state of excitement (and I advise giving them a "time out" in which to calm down, rather than to try to interact with and train them in that condition), but Salty would do it when he was calm. I figured out that Salty would tolerate a touch on his back, but touching him in the neck area triggered his aggression. I had seen a behavior-assessment video by Sue Sternberg that showed a four-month-old Rottweiler puppy acting exactly the same way, and it was presented as an example of deviant, aggressive behavior.

I described Salty's aggression on an email list of knowledgeable and insightful trainers. None of the trainers who replied was optimistic. Several had seen the Sue Sternberg video and found the Rottweiler puppy's behavior disturbing. Couldn't it be some kind of "phase," I asked. The other trainers thought that was wishful thinking.

I took stock. The alternatives were to keep the puppy, or to put him to sleep. (Dog owners have the option of returning a puppy to his breeder, but in this case I was the breeder.) He wasn't doing serious damage with his puppy teeth, so for the time being I kept him. I didn't think the "phase" idea was entirely wishful thinking. There was something in the sound of his growl, and the automatic nature of his response, that reminded me a lot of puppy play-fighting.

Salty now: gentle, cooperative, and affectionate.

To shorten a tale that is growing long, Salty outgrew his aggressive response to being touched. He outgrew his independence, becoming very affectionate, deeply attached, and eager to please. My friend Sue Alexander, who trains service dogs, came to visit and assessed him and told me, for her next Chesapeake she wants "a Salty." Teaching Salty to bring a retrieved object all the way back and deliver it was a big job, but now instead of ignoring me he looks me in the eye, sparkling all over, trying to figure out if he can make it a game.

Salty continued, for a few months, to stiffen if I touched him while he was eating. This is a level of resource guarding aggression that is considered acceptable in the breed, although it would be a concern in a home with owners who had no experience with it.

Once again, and contrary to the expectations of the best-informed people I could find, a puppy had grown out of his alarming behavior to become a good dog.

CHAPTER 2

OBEDIENCE

Why train your dog in basic obedience? The benefits are many, and important. A controllable dog causes less worry, and can be more fully integrated into family life. Through the training process, you come to better understand your dog, how he learns, what are his stumbling blocks, and how he is motivated. He comes to respect you and to trust that you will be fair, mean what you say, and acknowledge his effort. Thanks to the controllability and understanding established by training, behavior problems are easy to resolve or never occur in the first place.

There is more than one way to skin a cat, and there are many ways to train dogs. My goal in designing this program is to enable you to successfully train your dog, and for both of you to enjoy the process. Dog training is like dieting. It doesn't work if you treat it as something to endure in the short term, planning to put it behind you and get back to old habits. Learning never stops, and dogs readily learn whether the rules

Trained dogs can participate more fully in their owners' lives. This Dachshund spends the whole day with his owners at their service station.

have been relaxed. Like dieting, dog training works best if it has enough appeal for you to want to continue and incorporate it into your life with your dog long-term.

Research on learning tells us that we learn best by "positive reinforcement," for which I'm going to use the less precise "reward." Rewards don't just help us get the idea, they also motivate us to try again. This is true for us and for our dogs. I've tried to make the training process rewarding for the owner who follows it. Basing training on a walk, setting your dog up for success, and fostering a happy, cooperative attitude on the part of your dog are part of the program.

Planning on 10-minute training sessions can make it easier to fit training into your day. I strongly recommend making it a priority to get out with your dog every day, even if you have to shorten training to five minutes, or even just one. Maintaining continuity (and avoiding guilt feelings) is good for trainer motivation.

The original basis for recommending 10-minute training sessions was the recognition that dogs learn faster and make fewer mistakes when training sessions are not overlong. So keep it brief, enjoy your dog's enhanced learning, and don't feel compelled to schedule long, onerous sessions with your dog!

The obedience exercises are intended to be taught in sequence. The earliest topics are simple, involving only basic communication. They promote calm, uncontentious responses. They do not require an established training relationship; they lay out simple rules that an inexperienced dog can understand. A surprising amount of "bad behavior" is misunderstood communication. Diverse training methods start the same way: the trainer sets up a situation where the dog can work out simple cause and effect, while the trainer communicates little or nothing directly. Communication develops as training progresses, allowing trainer and dog to tackle more involved exercises.

Each exercise depends on the work that precedes it, and provides the foundation for later exercises in the sequence. Later, more complex commands depend on earlier ones in two ways. They combine concepts learned previously, and they depend on the training relationship that develops as you and your dog work through the exercises together. For the "down" exercise, for example, your dog must be ready to accept being placed in position by you, or else he will resist—and learn to keep resisting. For the "stay," your dog will already be familiar with waiting for a release command, making it simpler for him to learn to wait as you leave and return to him.

The progression begins with teaching your dog to walk politely and respond to the leash, or a longer line. Then we add "sit" and the release command "OK," followed by coming-when-called and the "stay" command. Next we teach walking at heel, returning to heel position at your left side, lying "down," on command, and finally the "stand." The last part of this section tells how to integrate training into everyday life and to keep your dog's responses reliable.

The method we will use is to first induce your dog to do the basics of an exercise, using a variety of influences, then to repeat and refine the exercise. Refining an exercise has two parts: polishing up your dog's initial, approximate response until he can do the exercise in its finished form, and gradually removing the inducements until he will respond to a verbal command or hand signal only. Repetition and praise will be our main teaching tools. We borrow heavily from modern, positive-reinforcement methods of training, in that we accept and praise efforts that may only approximate the finished exercise, knowing that we can gradually shape them up, and in relying on repetition and reward as our main tools of teaching.

We also borrow from more traditional methods, especially in the means we use to induce your dog to do a new exercise. My experience is that many owners find this approach intuitive.

Traditional training methods tend to routinely make use of corrections and/or punishment. I have trained many dogs this way, but I think there are compelling reasons to minimize punishment. Use of punishment in dog training has serious pitfalls. One is that it is often used ineffectively. Our culture is full of false notions about punishment and learning that set us up to punish ineffectively. What is ineffective punishment? It is simply harshness, often repeated, that achieves no benefit. I am sure that is not how owners wish to treat their dogs.

A second pitfall is that punishment tends to create an adversarial attitude. It is easier to do when angry, and plays into notions of "defiance" and "willfulness" and the old-fashioned idea that the dog is "bad." In the introduction to this book I go into more detail about what I see as a major problem with dog ownership in general—cultural notions that lead to adversarial, even paranoid attitudes toward our potential best friends. Use of punishment can push us in that direction.

Yet another pitfall of training with punishment is that while training we are trying to teach dogs to do something, and punishment is directed at stopping them from doing something. Punishment, to some degree, lends itself to stopping unwanted behavior, but not to encouraging a dog to try new things, or to continue trying after making a mistake. Finally, it is common for punishment to be misunderstood. Dogs may associate the punishment with something we don't intend, suddenly avoiding a situation, refusing to respond to a command, or becoming fearful.

I will give instructions on administering corrections in some circumstances. A "correction" combines an attention-getter with a prompt to do a desired action, and must be followed by praise when the dog completes (or approximates) the wanted action. The attention-getter may range from mild to physically harsh according to the dog's response. It should be no more than needed to get the dog's attention, and should never threaten or overwhelm him. Most dogs can complete the training sequence without physical corrections, but a few, typically the high-drive, confident, upbeat working type, may need them. Owners who use corrections must remember that dogs learn by repeating desired actions, not from harshness or punishment. Corrections should be seen as a tool to get your dog doing a desired action that has already been taught, and not as the central feature of training.

Corrections are only effective for a few things. Overall compliance depends on many features of the training program, including the sequence of exercises and the appropriate use of well-timed praise.

The sequence of training exercises takes into account an important feature of the way dogs react to us. Whenever we attempt to manipulate dogs physically, to push them around, they seem to take that as an invitation to resist. If the terms of the interaction are that we use force to try to make a dog do something, the dog interprets the rule as "whoever is stronger wins." Although we may prevail, we fail to teach what we intend. Dogs learn by association, and will associate the situation or the command given with the physical struggle. Instead of learning to do what we intend to teach, a dog is likely to conclude that vigorous contention is the appropriate response. Next time he will be more, rather than less, inclined to resist.

A familiar example occurs when we try to push down a jumping dog, only to elicit more vigorous jumping. Or when we take hold of a dog's collar to try to move the dog from here to there, and the dog struggles, perhaps ducking out of his collar, or else he lies on his back pushing us away with all four legs. Laying hands on a dog in these kinds of situations only makes things worse.

The solution to one of these impasses always involves standing back and finding a way to control the situation without touching the dog. It can be surprisingly easy; for example, a dog who struggles mightily against being pulled by the collar will come more willingly if we use a leash.

The sequence of training exercises calls for physically pushing your dog into a "sit," and taking hold of him to lay him "down." Preparation is needed in order for your dog to accept this physical manipulation. You start, very simply, at the end of a long line, asking little of your dog. Then, maintaining your distance and making the modest things you ask of your dog inevitable, you work through the low level of physical resistance associated with tension on the leash.

While this groundwork helps prepare your dog to accept the training for "sit" and "down," hands-off solutions are always the first choice when you feel the need to control your dog. Physically taking hold of your dog always costs you in terms of credibility, respect, and control. When you don't physically contend with him, your dog is more likely to respond willingly to gestures, body language, and commands he has learned.

At the end of the sequence of training exercises, I will describe how to incorporate the things your dog likes, including attention, food, and play opportunities, as rewards for performing commands. By doing this, you achieve control over your dog by controlling the things he wants. The section of this book on manners gives further ideas for using specific "real-life" rewards to encourage polite behavior.

While I hope this book will help you train your dog, I encourage you to take obedience classes if good ones are available. Classes provide motivation and camaraderie with other dog owners in the weekly get-togethers to show off what you've accomplished. In addition, a good instructor can do what a book cannot: help you read and respond appropriately to your individual dog.

Your class may use a method different from what I present. That's fine. You can adapt what is in the book to fit what your real-life instructor tells you. If your class uses clicker training, go ahead and introduce the exercises with a clicker, and then incorporate them into your training walk. In clicker training, you must eventually "diversify the rewards" in order to integrate your dog's training into daily life. Using praise, play, and free time on walks is a great way to begin diversifying. If your class uses luring (using treats to induce new behaviors), you can adapt it the same way. Introduce exercises according to the formalism used in class, and then practice them daily as you walk.

Perhaps you will enroll in a traditional type class. In that case, remember that even though the focus sometimes seems to be on corrections, repetition and reward still make up most of the learning process. Follow instructions carefully when administering corrections, and be sure to use praise, repetition, and free time to make your dog's overall experience a good one.

Here Are a Few Tips for Effective Training:

1. Pay Attention
Pay close attention to your dog. Dogs learn from well-timed feedback. They seem to be motivated by their trainer's attention, and discouraged if the trainer is inattentive. Frequent feedback is one of the keys to successful training, and if you are paying close attention, your expressions and body language supplement your commands and praise.

2. Use Praise
Remember that your dog is putting forth an effort to do as you direct. That effort must be acknowledged. Dogs are motivated by praise, as we are by thanks for our efforts. Effective praise is warm, but brief, and must be well-timed. Say "good!"

(or "yes!" or another word of your choosing) the instant your dog does as you ask. Excessive praise, which might go on and on, or be delivered in an excited tone of voice, tends to confuse dogs.

3. Build Credibility

Strive to build and maintain credibility. Trainers say, "never give a command you can't enforce." This means follow through on everything. If your dog does not respond properly, find a way to get control and make the command stick, going to get him if he doesn't come when called, for example. If he does respond, be sure to acknowledge his response with praise. Always remember to provide a clear finish to the "sit," "stay," "down," and "heel" commands.

Except in the teaching phase, where there is a possibility your dog didn't understand, don't repeat commands. Give them once and follow through. Repeated commands quickly lose their meaning.

4. End On a High Note

Try to end every training session with success. If your dog gives a best-ever performance on some exercise, definitely stop there! If you are having trouble getting a good result, don't keep pushing until you quit with your dog in a state of confusion. Simplify. Ask for less so that he has a chance to be successful. Don't worry that this means easing your standards. It's more important to end with a good response. On the other hand, there may be days when one or both of you get so rattled or confused you can't redeem the training session. Try to recognize these times, and when it is better to quit than to press on, take a break, then start with something simple and reassuring in the next session.

Some dogs make up games that can subvert the training process. One typical game is ducking away when you try to attach the leash. If your dog acts as though he enjoys his training walks, he is probably not afraid to go out with you. Try not to get angry. Dogs who do this are usually smart and interested in the training process. I see them as testing the boundaries, trying to learn how much control you have, how much latitude they have to invent things and have their own way, and whether you're committed to following through on what you ask them to do. Some of the best working dogs seem to want to make sure of their trainers' commitment before they will commit themselves.

To keep these games from getting out of hand, recognize that you control the situation—you don't have to grab your dog. Simply don't play along, because to do so would be rewarding to your dog. If he is ducking away from the leash, for example, don't go after him and try to take hold of his collar. Straighten up and wait for him to come to you. He wants to go out on his walk, after all. If he doesn't come, you can leave without him and, if you like, return and try again in five minutes.

In training, dogs normally expect us to move ahead with the lesson. Holding up training to wait for your dog to leave off playing some game he has invented amounts to withholding an expected reward. So don't fall for the games; don't go after your dog. Wait him out. Let him decide to drop the games in favor of moving forward.

Equipment

A few items of equipment will be needed for the training exercises: a collar, leashes and cords of different lengths, and a stick. Dogs can often be trained using buckle collars, which should be tight enough not to slip off over the dog's head. The slip

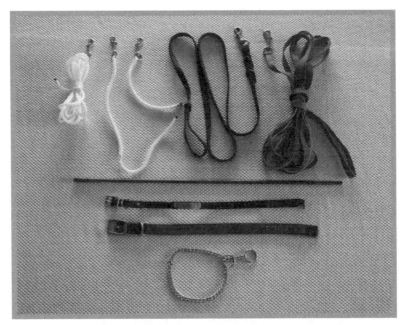

Basic training equipment. Top, left to right: Homemade long line, short cord, and tab, six-foot leather leash, 20-foot cotton longe line. Middle: training stick. Bottom, buckle collars and chain collar.

chain or "choke" collar is versatile. It is resistant to slipping off, and can be used to give a correction, if you have done the groundwork and find your dog is still inattentive.

There is a right way and a wrong way to put on the chain collar. When you reach the stage where your dog stays mainly on one side of you (the left side is traditional), make sure that the end of the chain to which the leash is attached passes through the ring and over the top of your dog's neck. The collar makes a letter "P" with the stem toward you and the loop downward. This will allow the collar to loosen immediately any time it

Right way to put a chain collar on a dog that walks on your left.

tightens. The shortest chain collar that will slip over your dog's head is the right length.

A six-foot leather leash is ideal for training. Other materials, such as cotton and especially nylon, are hard on the hands. Discomfort and difficulty holding the lead securely can lead to ineffective training. The six-foot length gives your dog enough room to do most of the exercises without tugs that may confuse him. It gives him some freedom to move around when walking on leash.

The longe line made from cotton webbing lets your dog get farther from you, and gives your dog a larger area in which to move. It is used for exercises that require distance between you and your dog, such as coming-when-called and stays at a distance, and for learning good leash manners. Longe lines were developed for training horses but are now readily available from pet-supply stores and catalogs as well as from feed stores and tack shops.

The training stick is used to help teach dogs to hold their position in the sit-stay and stand. It can help dogs learn heeling position and may also be used to give a reminder to dogs that respond slowly on "sit" even after many repetitions. There is nothing fancy about the stick. The one pictured is a section of fiberglass tent pole. Sticks can be cut from trees, or you can use a riding crop.

The homemade cords are used later in training. As you begin to transition to off-leash work, having your dog drag a long line enables you to catch him and follow through on a command that he might have ignored. We use braided polypropylene, which is lightweight and waterproof. The line has no loop on the end to snag. The polypropylene is hard on the hands, which makes it difficult to use in early training. It can cause rope burns, so when you need to catch a moving dog, step on the line, don't grab it in your hands.

The long line can be any length you like. As your dog becomes more reliable, you can shorten the cord bit by bit. The "short cord" shown is about two feet long, convenient for giving the occasional reminding tug to a dog that is under good control.

The "tab" is just a few inches long. It can be left attached to your dog's collar as a convenient "handle" should you need to guide him for any reason. Taking hold of a dog's collar introduces a new dynamic. Many dogs automatically resist or, at least, become distracted from the task at hand. Using a tab gets a much better result: dogs respond to it as they do to a leash. The tab is a useful tool for teaching your dog that obedience training applies everywhere. The one pictured is made from polypropylene braid; broken or chewed leashes can also be cut to tab length.

Polypropylene braid and bolt snaps can be bought at hardware stores and feed stores. Splicing the braid is easy, and instructions are usually printed on the package. It involves melting the ends over a candle to prevent fraying, and feeding one end down the hollow core of the braid. Bolt snaps with a swivel are best as they prevent twists from building up in your line. Choose brass or stainless steel bolt snaps.

A few specialty items, such as headcollars, harnesses, or a pinch collar may help with some dogs. Pictures and explanations will be included where appropriate.

You can get started with only a collar, leash, and longe line, and pick up the other items along the way.

Getting Started: The Training Walk

Training begins as taking a walk, something you and your dog can enjoy, and anticipate doing together. You will add requirements and obedience exercises a little at a time. This makes learning interesting to your dog but avoids overwhelming or confusing him, so he has little need to resist.

Walking together provides a reason for your dog to pay attention to you, connecting his actions and your responses. Early on, he will learn to respect the lead, and not pull against it. Once you begin, it is important to make sure you don't give him opportunities to pull at other times. This is essential! Any time a dog is on a taut lead, whether he pulls on you or you pull on him, the pulling habit is strengthened, or reinforced. When you need your dog to move from here to there, practice using body language and encouragement instead of force.

Help your dog develop a good attitude toward training by making the training walk a pleasant contrast with what goes on before. It is best if he is confined in a boring situation (such as a crate) for a couple of hours before you start. Be sure to give him an opportunity to air (relieve himself) before you get started.

Your dog should wear a secure collar, such as a buckle collar (not one with a plastic clip and a slide adjustment). A slip chain or "choke" collar, or even a pinch collar, might work better if you have a big, strong dog who otherwise ignores you.

Instead of a leash, attach a 15 or 20-foot line. I recommend the cotton webbing longe lines made for training horses. This extra-long "leash" will make it easier for your dog to learn the advantages of staying within the circle defined by a leash, by giving him a bigger target, and hence a greater success rate.

The ideal place for your walk is an open area, with few trees or other obstacles that can foul your longe line. You are going to allow your dog to be anywhere in the 15 or 20-foot circle defined by the line. Hold the line by the hand loop, and resist

Begin by going for a walk with your dog on the 15 or 20-foot longe line.

the temptation to grab the middle somewhere and take up slack or pull on your dog. Don't worry if your dog steps over the line or even gets wrapped in it. Most dogs quickly learn to get used to the sensation. If you have one of the rare panicky ones, you may need to shorten up the line and control it, but try to avoid holding it taut.

Adjusting to the Line

On your first walk, move at a relaxed pace and let your dog get used to the longe line, its weight, length, the way it catches on the ground and the sensations of getting it under a leg or over his body. Keep talking to a minimum, allowing your dog to concentrate on learning the ways of the longe line. There is no harm in going over ten minutes unless adapting to the line is stressful.

Repeat this relaxed walk with the longe line once or twice a day until it is comfortable for both of you. With some confident dogs this will happen in the first session. Many dogs need more time to explore the "rules" of suddenly getting brought up short any time they get 15 (20) feet from you, or to get used to the feel of the line.

Adapting to Your Movement

Once you and your dog are comfortable with the longe line, you now add the first requirement. You will go where you want to go, and your dog's 15 or 20-foot circle will move with you. Having learned that it's easier to be inside the circle, he will now learn to pay attention to you in order to keep up with it.

This time, before you begin walking, pick out a destination. Any landmark will do. Take the hand loop of the line securely in your hand and walk purposefully to the spot you have chosen. Leave your dog to his own devices. If you look at or speak to him, he may think his options include trying to influence you; you want him to learn to follow his circle as you move. Keep it simple and he will learn.

When you get to the spot you have chosen, pause for a minute. Pay attention to something other than your dog. When about a minute has passed, begin walking purposefully to a new destination. Repeat again and again for the duration of your training session.

Take "purposeful walks" for several training sessions, at least three or four. When your dog gets the picture, he will not drag behind or act confused, but he may try to challenge the boundaries by charging against the end of the line, or by forging ahead and towing you along. When he does this, or simply acts comfortable keeping up with you on the longe line, you are ready for the next step.

Learning Not to Pull

A dog that is pulling on his leash or line is not paying attention to you, and is therefore not ready to learn. When you physically restrain him, you relieve him of responsibility, and he is free to concentrate on other things and to leap, bark, and lunge at them. We use this principle in teaching puppies to retrieve. Restraining them encourages them to forget about us, and think only of that falling object they want to chase. In obedience training, we do the opposite. We want to eliminate the taut leash and get the dog paying attention to us. Going a step farther and teaching a dog to give to the lead, enables us to move him around with a feather touch, and to introduce some exercises by leading him through them.

To discourage your dog from pulling against the line, you will attach an unwanted consequence, that is, when your dog pulls, something will happen that he would prefer to avoid. It may take a little ingenuity to find the right consequence. Since pulling is a partly innate response, partly habit, and only partly intentional, dogs may not immediately connect the consequence you set up with their behavior. And because dogs vary in temperament, different consequences work for different dogs.

The first strategy I recommend is to stop walking as soon as your dog reaches the end of the line and starts to lean against its resistance. Establish the rule, "pulling gets you nowhere." Your dog may be eager to approach some person, dog, or object, or may be enjoying moving along at a brisk pace. Stopping thwarts his intentions either way. Stand still as long as he continues to pull forward. Eventually he will move in some direction that creates a little slack. In a calm voice, say "good," as you begin to walk forward once more.

The next time your dog starts to pull, again stop in your

tracks. It might be half a second after you begin to move. Wait until he slackens the lead, and then move forward again, calling attention to your change in response with a calm "good."

This strategy works with a lot of dogs. If you see improvement within the first few sessions, it is working. Because pulling is often an entrenched habit, it can take time to overcome. Try not to get angry if your dog's initial improvement is followed by many lapses. Give him the practice time he will need to replace the old habit with a good, new one.

Watch closely for your dog to reach the end of the lead, feel the slack disappear, and back off. Praise: "good boy!" every time this happens. He may acknowledge you with eye contact or a quick wag. This is the beginning of communication. Tell him "good!" again to reinforce this attention.

Some dogs don't connect your response (stopping) with their behavior (pulling). More emphatic consequences are needed. Frequently it is the big, energetic dogs, such as Labs, some German shepherds and other working breeds, who are predisposed to believe that they can make things happen by effort and action, not by holding back. Some dogs seem, by virtue of their size and weight, to think it is their prerogative to tow you around. They may patiently wait when you stop, but don't recognize it as a response to their pulling.

If your dog doesn't change his behavior in response to your stopping, strengthen your response. When he reaches the end of the line and leans into it, turn and go the other way. This is a bigger interruption and a more obvious failure of forward progress. Be ready for another turn any time your dog gets ahead of you with his attention on something else.

If you cannot go more than a few steps in any direction without your dog's charging ahead and pulling, he is still failing to get the message. You may need to get his attention before he will notice. An approach I have used with some of these dogs is to skip ahead in training, teaching the "sit" command and introducing recalls (coming when called). Then, every time your dog gets to the end of the lead and leans forward, call him, reel him in, and make him sit for a few seconds before releasing him. Most hard chargers will notice the contrast between free time and having to sit under control, and will learn what they have to do in order to maintain their freedom.

For the few that do not, a clear correction may be warranted. One option is to put a "choke" chain or, if he is physically insensitive, a pinch collar on him, and attach your longe line to it. Now, when he dashes past you intent on what is in front, quietly turn and go the other way. Try to "follow through" so that you keep moving past the point where he hits the end of the line and is brought up short. Don't look—make it his problem that he wasn't paying attention and going in the same direction you were.

Some of the more gung-ho pulling dogs will respond to training by turning to one side instead of pulling. They keep turning in one direction, so that they go around in a circle. This makes it difficult to stay clear of the long line. You can stop this by carrying a stick, three to four feet long, held out to one side. Shorten up the line so that the stick blocks your dog's path as he tries to circle.

From this point, episodes of pulling, that is, reaching the end of the line and leaning into it rather than backing off, should decrease, and instances where he responds by giving to the lead increase. Don't expect that because he's responded well once, he "knows" it. He's beginning to get the idea. Devote several walks to practicing.

When pulling is rare, and giving to the lead is the rule, your dog is ready to move on. If he is a persistent puller, move on anyway. After you have taught him to sit and to come when called, you can interrupt every attempt at pulling by calling him to you and making him sit. He will give it up.

Introducing "Sit" and "OK"

Our next objective is to introduce the "sit" command and the release command "OK," and to develop the value of praise as feedback telling your dog he got it right. You can use any sound you like as a release. Many trainers use "free," on the basis that we are less likely to confuse our dogs by using it in conversation.

Continue basing your training sessions on a walk, with your dog on the longe line. Now that your dog has graduated from the lesson on pulling, you can walk informally instead of intently from point to point.

During your walk, go to your dog, taking up the slack in the

"Sit" position.

line. Introduce "sit" by placing your dog in position. Hold the line at the clip attaching it to your dog's collar with your right hand, while you press down on his rear, just in front of his tail, with your left. Push him into a sitting position as you say, "sit."

As soon as your dog's rear touches the ground, say "good!" then "OK!" as you release your hold and give him three or four feet of slack in the line. All you are asking of him at this point is to allow you to push him into a sit. That's plenty without requiring him to stay there. Praise for complying should be immediate.

After a few seconds of "free time," repeat. Do a few repeti-

Hold the line at the clip to keep your dog's head up and keep him from moving forward, as you press down on his hindquarters to push him into a sitting position.

tions, then continue your walk. Have several sessions of work on "sit," for a total of 20-25 repetitions on your 10-minute walk.

After a few repetitions, if your dog lingers in a sitting position, pat him in the ribs and move forward, giving a forward tug on the lead, as you say "OK!"

A dog must understand the release command if he is to be reliably obedient. It helps him understand commands that have a duration, that is, that he is expected to keep doing until told otherwise. If you are having trouble getting your dog to release, include fewer repetitions of "sit" and more free time in between, and be animated as you encourage him to release.

Within a few sessions, your dog will begin to sit in response to your spoken "sit!" and the touch of your hand on his rear. Begin to give the command "sit," an instant before prompting the sit with your hands on his rear and the clip at his collar. As he shows less need of these prompts, make them lighter. Any time he sits more quickly than usual, or in response to less pressure, let some extra warmth into your voice as you praise.

The goal is to get him sitting in response to the command without needing a physical prompt. Normally you can abandon the pressure on the rear first, but may still need to give a reminding pull upward on his lead occasionally. As he progresses, a little tug is adequate, with no need to reach down and take hold of the clip.

Patting the dog in the ribs encourages him to get up as you say, "OK!"

When your dog no longer needs to be pushed into position, and you are using less and less prompting, you can begin teaching him to hold the position for a moment before getting up. All you have to do is delay the release command. Don't wait too long—a second is about right.

Be ready to use your hands to prompt him back into position if he starts to get up before your release. When he responds by sitting back down, promptly release and praise him. This timing helps him understand that the verbal commands, "sit" and "OK," are the key to what he is to do when.

If that goes well, delay a little longer. One and a half, then two seconds.

Pet your dog and talk to him calmly ("what a good boy"),

Your hands keep him in place while working to convince him that it's good to remain there.

as you hold him in place. Then when you release him, stop. Free time has its attractions, but he will be learning the right responses to commands earn him your attention.

When increasing duration on any command, increments of fifty percent work well. If your dog remains in place for one second, your next target may be one and a half. If he stays for five seconds, one and a half times that is seven and a half. You could shoot for seven, then when he's mastered that, work for ten, which is not quite one and a half times seven.

When increasing duration, do not make every repetition the same. After your dog stays for your target time, give him a shorter, easier "sit" to ensure success and promote confidence. The average time you ask him to stay will be increasing, but some repetitions will be short and easy, while some will be longer, up to the new target. With practice, one target will become the average time he stays, and you will be working on a new target.

When your dog sits in response to a light touch and will remain sitting, receiving attention for five seconds and more (until released), he is ready to add a new exercise: coming when called.

Continue working on "sit," increasing the time your dog will sit waiting for a release, and decreasing his dependence on prompts and continuous petting while he sits. Since staying in place for a long time is relatively boring, do fewer repetitions as you ask him to sit for longer periods, interspersing "sits" with more active exercises—such as coming when called.

Introducing "Here"

The objective of this section is to teach your dog the action of coming and sitting by you, in response to your command, under controlled conditions. Reliable recalls, where your dog will always listen for your call, immediately drop whatever he is doing and return to you, will come later.

Begin your walk as usual, using the longe line. Once you are on your way, wait for your dog to get some distance from you, then call him. You will do several things at once.

When he is a few feet from the end of the line, say his name and "here!" as you begin moving away from him. If you can walk or run backwards, great. Otherwise look at him over

"Here" command.

your shoulder as you move away. He is already used to forced changes of direction, and should move toward you. In addition, dogs are naturally inclined to move toward someone who is moving away.

Say "good boy" as soon as your dog turns toward you or if he starts to move. Take up the line as he moves closer, and keep taking it up until he is right in front of you. Now get a hold of the line near his collar and say "sit!" as you gently prompt him with an upward pull.

As soon as he is sitting, give him praise and attention as you have been doing on the "sit." After a few seconds, tell him "OK." Resume your walk.

Call your dog as you start to back away. Be sure to praise him when he turns toward you.

Try to take up the line, and continue moving backward as your dog comes toward you.

Reach down and take hold of the line near your dog's collar to prompt him to sit.

Repeat this sequence as often as you can on your walk. With many dogs, you can get in lots of practice for a day or two, but then they start watching you and don't often get far enough away for you to call. This is good in its own way!

If you were not able to get your dog to stop pulling in his earlier lessons when walking on a long line, you now have an additional tool to help you. Time your practice on coming-when-called so that any time your dog gets to the end of the line and begins to pull, you immediately call him. As before, praise him as he turns, move backward (or away from him), reel him in, and make him sit. The consequences of pulling are now a greater interruption of his explorations than before.

This kind of dog ordinarily gives you opportunities to practice coming when called, and with all this practice, learns both to come on command and to refrain from pulling.

Keep practicing "sit," with intervals of relaxed walking as well as practicing coming when called. Decrease the attention you give your dog while he is sitting. Change to low-key verbal praise, and praise at intervals during a longer sit, but not continuously.

As you decrease praise during the "sit," add a warm "good boy" following the "OK" release.

Continue practicing recalls as you teach new exercises. As your dog's response improves, reduce your movement away from him as you call, changing the emphasis to your verbal command, and away from the invitation to chase you.

As your dog learns the game and comes in faster, you may not be able to take up the line fast enough. That's OK; just reach down to take hold of the line to prompt him to sit.

A little clumsy, but we got there.

"Stay" command.

Introducing "Stay"

By this time, your dog has learned to pay attention to you, especially when you are moving away. He also knows how to hold the "sit" position for a few seconds and wait for the "OK" release. Now you will draw upon these skills and ask him to pay attention as you move away, while holding still in the "sit" position.

Begin your training walk as before. Practice a recall or two if your dog will still get far enough away for you to do so. Walk a bit further and practice the "sit"/"OK" sequence a few times. Give your dog a few moments' break, then introduce the new exercise.

Get into position with your dog more or less at your left

side. Tell him "sit," and give an upward tug on the lead whether he needs it or not. Tell him "good boy," but do not pet him. Now you will do several things at once.

Maintain a slight upward pull on the lead as do the following. Give a cautionary gesture with your right hand in front of your dog's face and say "stay" in a calm voice as you step in front of him and pivot to face him, with your knees in front of his nose. The hand gesture seems to help dogs focus and respond appropriately. Perhaps it tips them off that something new is expected.

Do not stay for very long in front of your dog. Half a second will do. A successful completion of the "stay" will let him know what is expected, but if you dawdle and he gets up, it may be a long time before he understands.

Say "good" in a calm voice, then step back by his side. Now praise more warmly and release him.

That's all it takes to introduce the "stay." Practice it a few times, keeping his stays brief to ensure his success. When he appears to know the routine, which may require five repetitions or a couple of sessions' work, begin to increase the duration of his stays using the 50% rule described in the section on "sit."

Success and reliability in obedience training depend on the trainer's ability to hold his or her dog's attention. Techniques to build attention, such as including a variety of exercises in the course of a walk, are incorporated into this obedience sequence. Having introduced "stay," you now have more tools

Give a cautionary gesture with your right hand as you step forward.

Stand close in front of your dog, giving him minimal temptation to move.

to help promote attention. As you extend the amount of time your dog will "stay," praise and reward him for paying attention. You will keep him from being bored, and motivate him to listen carefully to verbal commands, by mixing up exercises so he can't anticipate what's coming next. And finally, you will help him develop discipline and focus by remembering to finish each exercise with an "OK" release.

Once you have your dog staying for a couple of seconds or more, begin praising him when he makes eye contact. This may be rare at first, as dogs often look everywhere but at the trainer when learning to stay. If he glances up at you briefly, say "good boy," and immediately step back by his side and praise again. If you were planning to make him stay 10 seconds and he looked up at you after three, that's fine. Remember training goes faster when short stays are mixed in with longer ones, and you want him to have his reward for making eye contact.

If your dog starts looking at you so much that you aren't getting to practice any longer stays, great! Work on improving eye contact, increasing the standard the same as for the "stay" itself. Require that he maintain eye contact for half a second before you praise and step back. Then increase it a tiny bit more. Pretty soon he will be looking at you for several seconds, and you will be back to working on lengthening his "stays," but with good eye contact throughout.

Avoid boring your dog. Keep training interesting by continuing your walk and practicing some recalls in between sessions on "stay" lasting perhaps a minute or two.

Eye contact on sit-stay.

Once your dog will stay for ten seconds while you stand
with your knees in front of his nose, it's time to start working
on distance. Next time you tell him to "stay," step to a spot a
couple of inches farther in front of him than usual. Make it a
brief stay. Dogs learn best when you work on a single element
of challenge at a time, so keep duration short as you build distance. Use the 50% rule. Any time your dog is comfortable
with you at a given distance, vary the distance you move away
using the "comfortable" distance as an average, a maximum of
50% more than that, and a few close, easy ones mixed in.

Once you achieve reliable stays as you go some distance
away and return, begin to gradually build duration at that
distance. Adjust progress so that your dog is successful almost

Stroke, tap, and gently push your dog with the stick.

100% of the time. He will learn much more from his successes than from failure. If he gets up and comes toward you, take him back to where he was sitting, sit him back down, step away briefly, step back, praise him, and end the exercise.

Another technique for building your dog's concentration and reliability is to add a little controlled distraction on these stays. From two or three feet away, touch him gently on the shoulder with a training stick as he sits and stays. Chances are he will show a little uncertainty but will stay in place. Praise him if he does! Continue to incorporate touches from the stick into your stay exercises, working up to a firmer tap on the shoulder. You can also stroke him gently with the stick on the back, head, and legs. This exercise introduces the rule that little things that happen aren't an excuse to jump up and ignore training.

Never forget that longer and longer stays are more and more BORING. Fortunately they give you a new means of being unpredictable. You can now call your dog from a stay, and you might do it at any second! But he can't just jump up and run to you, because you might be planning to walk back to his side. Recalls are more fun for him, but be sure to return to him some of the time, or you will find he will lose his "stay."

If you want good, long, reliable stays of several minutes, you must counteract the boredom. Don't do too many in a session. Consider giving your dog a special reward after a good, long stay. This could be a treat, or it could be a game of chase or tug, or a retrieve. And, of course, training should always include walking and other exercises as well as stays.

Introducing "Heel"

To "heel," or walk at heel, means for your dog to walk calmly at your side, without breaking from position or sniffing the ground. Traditionally dogs heel on the left side, and sit without an additional command when their handler stops walking. A fresh "heel" command is given when you start forward. Unless you want to enter obedience competition, you are free to teach your dog to heel on the right if you prefer. Just reverse left and right in the instructions.

Heeling is just modified walking. You and your dog will start by heeling just a few steps, and gradually add all of the

"Heel" command.

details. You have already established the groundwork—your dog moves with you, gives to the lead, sits on command (with or without additional cues such as an upward tug), and, with the "stay" exercise, has learned to concentrate on doing as instructed for a period of time.

To begin, get into position with your dog sitting on your left. Hold your lead with some slack, so that you won't be tugging on your dog as you walk, but will be able to give him a reminder to sit, if needed, without pulling the lead in hand over hand. The ideal way to hold the leash is with either the thumb or all fingers of your right hand through the hand loop. Adjust the amount of slack you give your dog by making a loop out of the length of the leash and grasping that in the palm of

Starting position for heeling.

your right hand. When you need to give a tug as a reminder to your dog, use both hands, closing your left hand on the looped leash just below your right hand, as if you were gripping a baseball bat.

Say your dog's name and "Heel!" as you step forward with your left foot (i.e. the foot closest to him). As he gets up and moves with you, say "good." Promptly, before he can think of anything other than coming with you, stop and say "sit." I typically go for one second. If necessary, give him an upward tug as a reminder to sit. Tell him "good!" the moment his rear touches the ground.

This is the basic exercise. Repeat, being sure to include well-timed praise. Don't worry if your dog tightens the leash

Start out by stepping forward with your left foot as you say your dog's name and "heel."

by starting to get ahead of you or veering out to the side. He will get the idea with repetition. After about five repeats, give your dog an "OK" and a break. Continue your walk informally before practicing again. This will help your dog to associate the new rules with the "heel" command, and understand that he doesn't have to walk like that all of the time.

Use of your dog's name when a command requires him to move is traditional, probably for good reason. It gets his attention and lets him know some action is required. By contrast, tradition is not to use dogs' names with stationary commands such as sit, stay, and down. Always use the "heel" command when you begin moving with your dog, even if you were just heeling and he sat without a command.

On your walk, stop and practice "heel" at this level three or four times. Also include practice on "here" and "stay."

Introducing heeling with very short duration helps establish that it's a time for your dog to pay attention to you. You can increase this effect by including some variations that will keep him focused. Occasionally start off very fast, and stop suddenly. Give a warmer than usual "good boy!" when he is clearly attentive and puts the effort into staying with you. Praise for effort at this point. Your dog doesn't yet know what the point is, but "paying attention and staying with you" is a game he can learn.

Once your dog is starting and stopping well, increase duration as with "stay." Go two seconds, then start applying the 50% rule. Remember this means including shorter-than-average stretches of heeling as well as some of up to 150% of the distance at which your dog is reliable.

A few dogs are very slow to get the idea of walking next to you, and will charge ahead any time you try to go more than a few steps. You can help such a dog get the idea by holding your training stick in front of him, blocking his way. Hold the stick in your right hand, and the leash in your left. Practice this for several days, praising your dog as he walks in place and as he sits, then try it without the stick. There are dogs who will just push the stick aside and keep going. If yours is one of these, you can shape him up by making quick about-turns.

You and your dog may already be familiar with this concept, as dogs that will bull past a training stick are frequently the same dogs who required an about turn to learn to walk politely

Using a training stick to help a dog understand where to walk at heel.

on a slack lead. When heeling, your turn needs to be more tightly choreographed. If your dog is on your left, and you are holding your leash in your right hand as described at the beginning of this section, you will make your turn when your left foot is forward. Pivot to your right until you are facing the opposite direction, now with your right foot forward. Stride forward boldly in the new direction with your left foot. As you do this, let go of the loop of leash grasped in your palm, and hold the hand loop of your leash firmly against your body with both hands. Brace yourself, keep going, and don't look back. If your dog was so inattentive as to be left behind, you want him to perceive your change of direction as inevitable, not negotiable. When he catches up to you on your left side, praise him.

He responded to events by paying attention and making an effort to get into position, just as you want him to.

As you heel, watch your dog! When he looks at you, whether he makes eye contact or turns his head to look at your legs, praise him, saying "good." If you see him deliberately adjust his position, praise a him more warmly, saying "good boy!" This is what you want him to do, so you must give him feedback that lets him know.

As you heel together for longer periods of time, your dog will have more opportunities to wander out of position. At some point he will, but don't worry; you don't need perfection at this stage. The important thing is for your dog to pay attention and move with you. If he gets more than 1½ feet ahead or behind, or 2½ feet out to the side, you can begin teaching him that position is important. Give a quick tug with the lead and say "eh!" Thanks to his previous training, your dog should give to the lead and move toward your side. IMMEDIATELY praise this effort: "Good boy!" Stop and sit your dog, with praise, before he can get out of position again.

Once you begin correcting for position, it is your responsibility to strike a balance that will help your dog learn. Multiple corrections are likely to confuse him. Most dogs learn faster when they can contrast getting it right with the consequences of making mistakes. Heel your dog for shorter distances to maintain a high success rate. Make sure your dog does not get a correction more than one time in three.

In addition, make sure that you only correct when he is out

of position by at least the distances given above. Perhaps the biggest mistake in teaching heeling is to nitpick for minor position errors. You don't want to give your dog the idea that he is wrong when he is close to you; it will undermine his confidence. At this stage, success is staying on your left side without running off. Later I'll describe how to refine position without nitpicking.

Most dogs really like heeling. It's like a game to them—a challenge to see if they can pay adequate attention and not get caught out by a sudden action on the handler's part. Be sure to make it interesting. As with the sit-stay, be unpredictable. Speed up, slow down, speed up, stop suddenly. Praise your dog for effort and sharp responses.

When you see your dog making an effort to stay with you, make heeling even more interesting by incorporating turns. A sudden right turn and a quick step away give you a chance to catch your dog lagging behind. If he quickens his pace, praise him as he catches up.

If you make a sudden left turn, you might bump into your dog. Say "oops!" in a sympathetic but cheerful voice. Always praise when your dog responds to a maneuver or change of pace, even if he gets caught by the leash or you stumble in to him first. Good timing enhances any praise; the moment to praise is when he catches up to proper position.

As your dog gains confidence and enthusiasm, vary the game to try to catch him off guard. Try heeling in a straight line at a moderately slow pace, acting a little uninterested yourself, even "forgetting" to praise. Watch for your dog's attention to wander, then make a quick right turn and break into a trot! Praise him when he catches up to you, even if he got caught napping. This will lead him to take a uniform pace, or seeming inattention from you, as a reminder to keep concentrating.

Most dogs want to sniff the ground occasionally as they are walking, and it is difficult communicating to them that "heeling" involves keeping their heads up. Punishment for sniffing is particularly inappropriate, because when dogs get worried, they tend to hold their heads low. They may even sniff the ground as a strategy to defuse antagonism.

Making a game of heeling and attention provides a useful context for getting dogs to heel with their heads up. Ground-sniffing can be discouraged indirectly as a failure to pay attention. I find a quick stop and "sit!" command is the most productive response. Watch your dog as the two of you heel along, so that you can stop the instant his nose goes to the ground. Tell him "sit" with a correction—make him think he was inattentive and slow. Then pause for several seconds before you move on. This is boring. Boredom, and interruption of the game, is the consequence that will reduce your dog's inclination to sniff.

Besides being useful to correct ground-sniffing, a "sit" correction can be used to speed up your dog's sits if he is slow in sitting, despite your animated style and well-timed praise. There are two ways to do it. Most dogs respond to a quick, upward snap or jerk of the lead, made using a two-handed grip. This is more effective using a chain "choke" collar rather than a buckle collar; the collar should make a "zip" noise. This echoes the prompt you used when you taught your dog to sit, but adds an abrupt, attention-getting quality. Do it as you stop and give the "sit" command, not afterward. Remember to praise immediately when your dog sits.

For dogs that don't improve in response to an upward snap of the lead, a smart tap on the rear with the training stick will usually work. Carry the stick ready under your left arm while holding the leash in your left hand. As you stop and say "sit," apply upward tension on the lead as you strike your dog's rear smartly with the stick. The tension on the lead helps your dog respond correctly, while the stick may more effectively get his attention than the jerk on his collar. It is important to praise immediately when his rear goes down.

Stashed under your left arm, the stick does not intimidate your dog, but is ready when you need it.

If your dog is slow to sit, you can give him a sharp tap on the rear.

Once your dog clearly understands sitting promptly, staying with you and paying attention, you can work to refine his position. You will start responding to smaller errors of position on his part, but not by nagging him. Instead, speed up when he gets a little bit behind, and verbally encourage him to catch up. Slow down when your dog starts to get ahead of you. A dog that is impatient will learn that he can keep you moving by controlling himself and staying in position.

As I said earlier, your dog will quickly become discouraged and confused if you start giving corrections for small errors. You can tighten up the heeling position, whether your dog strays too far out to the left, forward, or behind, by exaggerating his error and then correcting. If your dog is too far to the left, for example, take a quick step to the right so that his incorrect position is really obvious, and snap the leash sharply while saying "heel." By "snap the leash," I mean give a quick jerk that takes up the slack and causes the chain collar to make a "zip" sound. The idea is not to yank, pull, or force your dog into position, but to get his attention and add emphasis as you point out his error.

If your dog tends to get ahead of you, make a sudden stop and tell him to "sit." If he is slow to sit, sharpen his response with sit corrections as described above. After a few repetitions he will stay closer beside you where he can better watch to see when you are stopping.

When your dog lags behind you, quickly stride out so that he is much farther behind than usual before correcting. After a small number of corrections, your dog should take your increase in pace as a cue that he needs to concentrate and keep up.

A few dogs persistently lag behind and do not respond to corrections of the kind I've described. Typically this occurs when a dog does not enjoy the game. The most satisfactory solution would be to shorten sessions and lower standards so that your dog has a higher ratio of success. When your dog again acts like an eager participant, gradually raise standards once more.

Teaching your dog to heel in a figure-eight can further polish his heeling position. The figure-eight is also one of the exercises in AKC Novice Obedience, in which dogs can demonstrate their attentiveness while heeling. It involves walking in a figure-eight pattern between and around two objects or "posts," which may be trees, cones, chairs, or whatever is convenient. In obedience classes, two classmates with their dogs seated at heel are often used as posts.

When you walk in a figure eight, on one loop your dog is on the outside and must move smartly in order to keep up, while on the other he is on the inside and has to walk slowly to avoid getting ahead of you. You can help refine his abilities by exaggerating the challenge. Speed up when your dog is on the outside, and slow down when he is on the inside.

In competition, handlers begin the figure-eight exercise facing the spot halfway between the two posts (which will be two people) from about five feet away. They begin walking on the judge's command and may be told by the judge to "halt" at any time. It makes sense to practice the same way. Going around the right side of the figure-eight first puts your dog on the outside, requiring him to speed up for the first part of the exercise. This is better for his attentiveness, instead of starting out on the slow left side. Heel your dog around the two posts, sprinkling in a number of unexpected stops.

This book is not specifically about preparing you and your dog for competition, but be aware that in the ring you are expected to heel your dog at an even pace, except when told by the judge to speed up and slow down. Points are deducted for the handler who adapts to his or her dog; your dog is expected to adjust his pace to yours. The changes of pace recommended here are for training purposes, to build your dog's attention and accuracy.

Returning or "Finishing" to Heel Position

At this point it is easy to teach your dog the other part of the "heel" command, which is to come to the heel position. I prefer a "flip finish" where your dog comes to your left, turns toward you, making a small circle on your left side, and sits down in heel position, facing forward. This avoids having your dog walk behind you, breaking the connection of mutual attention.

As with other commands, you will start by making the action as obvious and easy as possible, then refine it. Your dog now understands walking with you and yielding to the leash, allowing you to guide him into position. You will use your movements and the leash to teach him to track your left leg as you move backward and forward, and then you will reduce the amount you move, bit by bit, until you need only give a command (and a hand signal if you like) and your dog will make a neat circle and sit at heel.

You will face in the same direction as you move around in this exercise. Begin with your dog in front of you. Bunch up the leash in your left hand, holding it at a point about 1½–2 feet from your dog. Now hold your left hand out to your left, guiding your dog to accompany you on your left as you say "let's go," and start to walk backward. When you get him moving, tell him "good," and go backward a few steps. Then, as you continue to face forward, take a step to the right, encouraging your dog to turn toward you, and walk forward, telling him "heel." When you arrive near your starting point, stop and sit your dog, and praise him warmly.

Begin with the dog in front, left hand to the side, right hand patting thigh. The dog's tongue shows her uncertainty at this new situation.

As your dog follows you backward, you will be on his left, whereas he is used to your being on his right when he is heeling. This is new and different, so be patient with him as he works it out. You can pat your left thigh with your right hand to encourage him, continuing to guide him with the leash in your left. Tell him "good" when he takes a step in the right direction.

Practice a few times, then continue your walk and review other exercises. When your dog is smoothly accompanying you backward and forward, you can begin to reduce the distance that you move. Soon, a single step back on your left foot, accompanied by a gesture to the side with your left hand guiding him around, will be enough to get him to circle and sit

Keep going back several steps while your dog gets the idea of this new kind of heeling.

As you start to walk forward, your dog will turn toward you.

Ah, now this part is familiar.

Good dog.

in position. Now you can give a single command, "heel," as you begin the exercise. Further practice will allow you to eliminate the step backward, keeping only the gesture with your left hand, and the "heel" command.

Once finishing to heel from in front of you has been mastered, your dog can easily learn to come to heel position from a sit-stay off to one side or behind you. Just practice. Always praise when he sits neatly in place.

Your training sessions at this stage should still involve a walk, with stops along the way to practice all of the exercises your dog has learned: Sitting at your side; staying as you walk away and return; being called from a sit-stay; heeling with stops, turns and changes of pace; practice on the "finish;" and clear ends to exercises, using "OK!" or another release command, followed by stretches of informal walking.

You can add a fun variation of a recall, called a "chase recall." Whether you surprise your dog by calling him during the casual part of your walks, or call him from a "stay," once in awhile call him and run as fast as you can in the opposite direction. Praise him when he catches you and gently insist that he "sit," even though he is excited. Occasional opportunities to chase you will improve his attention and sharpness of response.

Introducing "Down"

The objective of this exercise is to teach your dog to lie down on command, and to relax and remain in place when told to "stay."

"Down" command.

The ability to get your dog to lie down on command is useful in any circumstance where he is in the way or may intimidate anyone. You can also use the command to improve your dog's manners in the home, easily putting a stop to activities such as begging at the table or pestering visitors.

"Down" comes late in the sequence because of its potential for resistance on the part of your dog. My preferred method of teaching it is to lift and place a dog in the position. This works only if your dog will relax and willingly allow you to manipulate him. Training up to this point should have built up trust and tolerance, but a few dogs will still resist. Avoid getting into a tussle with your dog! That will set back his responsiveness in all areas—even if you win.

If your dog resists strenuously, you can try luring him into position with food, develop a program to progressively teach him to accept being manipulated, wait for him to lie down and give him his favorite reward, or skip the exercise.

Most dogs will allow you to place them in the "down" position, and after a few days' worth of repetitions, will begin lying down on their own with no corrections needed.

Before you start to work on "down," begin your training walk and practice the exercises your dog responds to most willingly. Stop in a place with soft, mown grass if possible, and get him into a sit at your side. Stroke him on the back and side of his neck, telling him "good boy," then kneel beside him. Rub his chest and speak to him soothingly. Usually you can see your dog relax. Place him in the down position as shown in the photo below.

Bunch up the leash in your left hand, so that you hold it at

When your dog is relaxed, gently place him in the "down" position.

the clip and your elbow extends over your dog's back. Reach behind his right foreleg and grasp his left foreleg a little below the elbow with your right hand. Lift both forelegs with your right hand and arm, and using your left arm on his back to discourage him from getting up, lift his front end forward and down to place him in a natural lying-down position.

As soon as you get his elbows onto the ground, tell him "good" in a warm, but calm voice, and gently release him, saying "OK." It is fine if he gets right up. As always, we will build duration after getting him comfortable with the beginnings of the exercise.

If your dog resisted a little bit, but you did a good job of praising and letting him up as soon as his elbows touched, you can expect him to improve with repetition. He will notice that things get better—he gets released—as soon as he allows you to place his elbows on the ground.

After placing your dog "down" just once, continue your walk for a short time (ten seconds to half a minute). Repeat the sequence. After placing him in the "down" position about five times, with short walks in between, review another exercise briefly, then repeat the "down" and walk sequence about five more times.

Continue including the "down" exercise in your training sessions in this manner until your dog is willing and relaxed about letting you place him in a down, and does not seem anxious to get up. Now start to delay the "OK," remembering to praise as soon as you get him on the ground. As when you were first working on "sit," pet and praise your dog gently while he is in the lying-down position, but cease this attention when you give him the "OK" release.

Do not make your dog stay in position too long. Four or five seconds is about right for most dogs. Keep practicing at this level and, as with the "sit," you will probably notice your dog beginning to melt into a "down" position as you get ready to place him. See if you can prompt him to lie down with gentle downward pressure on the lead close to his neck. Do not get into a pulling match. If he resists, more pulling will create more resistance. Go back to placing him as necessary.

Most likely, you will be able to decrease and eliminate physical manipulation just as with "sit," or more easily. A downward hand gesture with the right hand, the intuitive traditional signal for "down," will help.

Once he is going down without your touching him, begin work on "stay." This should be easy, as he learned "stay" in connection with "sit," and lying down is a more relaxed position for most dogs. Within a short time you should be able to get him to lie down and stay for as long a time, with you as far away, as you've practiced on "sit."

Many dogs, once they start relaxing on the "down" exercise, don't get up immediately on being released. A good solution is to follow a down-stay with another exercise. Return to your dog, standing so that he is at your left side. Pick up his lead, say his name and "heel," then step forward a few steps, sit him and praise him before giving him an "OK!"

It is important to continue practicing "sit" and sit-stays, so that your dog doesn't come to think that all sits lead to downs. If he starts to lie down on sit-stays, the easiest remedy is to shorten the duration so that he is doing it right. Practice, then gradually increase again.

If his rate of success is high, your dog can learn from mistakes. When he lies down, go to him, lift him into a sit, give a firm "stay," walk away for an instant only, then return to him and finish the exercise. If he is lying down much of the time, however, he will not learn from this routine, so it is essential to shorten his stays to get him doing it right.

Stand

The one remaining exercise that's included in AKC Novice Obedience is the "Stand for Examination," where your dog stands still, without moving his feet, while you step away and a stranger (the obedience judge) comes over and touches him on the head, shoulders, and rear. The value of the "stand" exercise is that it makes it easier to groom and examine your dog, and to do things such as soak his hind feet if that should ever be necessary. The exercise comes at the end of the sequence, because it depends on the cooperation that you have built through the previous exercises. It will further develop cooperation, communication, and your dog's trust in you.

The biggest obstacle to learning the "stand" is your dog's prior work emphasizing "sit." Most dogs require practice and patience to learn that it's really OK to stay on their feet. Be

"Stand" command.

patient as you work through this. In the end, your dog will have a better understanding of "sit," as well as "stand."

Begin with your dog in his now-familiar position on your left. Look at him. His front and hind paws are close together. In order to get to his feet, either his front feet must move forward or his hind feet must move back. Forward is easier. Take a step forward with your right foot while using the leash to gently guide your dog forward, just far enough to get him to his feet, as you say "stand." The moment your dog is on his feet, say "good!" in a warm, enthusiastic voice. Before he can move or sit back down, give him a pat on the ribs and an "OK" release. Wait a few seconds, then repeat.

Practice this over and over again, looking for signs your dog recognizes what you want. When you think you see them, begin working on getting him to remain standing for a moment, just as you did with "sit." Pause before releasing him, and slowly increase the length of the pause, using the 50% rule. Remember to vary the length of time he remains standing—don't just make the pauses uniformly longer and longer. Watch your dog for signs he is about to sink back into a "sit." Reach down and, with a gentle hand under his belly, constrain him to remain standing. Praise him when he responds to your adjustment by standing back up.

When your dog is comfortable standing at your side for a few seconds, tell him to "stay" and step out in front of him. Praise softly, step back by his side, praise again, and release him. Now increase the length of the stay and your distance from him, as you did with the sit-stay and down-stay. If he has trouble understanding that he is to stay behind, have him stand on something like a pallet or the edge of a porch, so that a move forward would be a big step down.

If you train with treats, shaping up the "stand" is an opportunity to make good use of them. As your dog stays with you out front, step up to him and give him a treat, then step back. If you can catch him standing squarely with his head up, the treats will reinforce that good posture.

Use your training stick to begin teaching your dog to hold his position despite being touched. At first touch your dog lightly on the shoulders. As he gets used to this, touch and stroke him on the back, head, and legs. Teach him to hold his position in response to pressure by pushing lightly with the stick and prais-

If your dog starts to sink into sitting position, gently lift him up again so he is standing.

Pressing gently on his back makes him brace himself and remain standing.

Standing at the edge of the porch helps him understand he is not to step forward.

ing him as he stands. Condition him to resist as you push harder. You should be able to push him without hurting him.

Next, touch your dog with your hands. Start lightly and be sure to praise him for standing. He is used to responding to you and needs to know what you want. Touch his head and back. Press lightly on his rear and praise if he resists the pressure. Condition him to resist more pressure.

If your dog is still moving his feet while on his stand-stay, begin using verbal corrections ("ah!"). Now that he knows a touch is not an invitation to break his stay, you can position his feet. Stand at his right side. Position his left front foot by reaching over his back and grasping his foreleg at the elbow. Gently move the leg until his paw is in the right place. Press gently on

Using a stick to teach a dog to be more focused as he stands.

his withers to encourage him to keep his leg where you have placed it. Place his hind legs one at a time, grasping them just below the hock joint. Do shorter stays for awhile, aiming for success on keeping feet still until released.

Now find a helper. Put your dog on a stand-stay with you out in front. On your signal, your helper is to approach your dog without speaking, touch his head, and calmly walk away. From your position in front, watch your dog and praise when he makes eye contact with you, and when he shows any visible effort to resist temptation to move. Return to your dog, warmly praise, and release him.

When your dog responds well to your helper's approach, have him or her touch your dog's shoulders and back/rear as

Placing a dog's hind foot.

well as his head. This is what a judge would do in the obedience ring. You can, if you like, go further and condition your dog to be touched all over, to be groomed, to have his feet handled, or to have his teeth and testicles examined as in the show ring. It's up to you. Just build gradually, and continue to practice the stand exercise around distractions, as described later in this section.

Transition to Off-Leash Work

By the time you have taught your dog all of the exercises, he is probably paying pretty good attention and enjoying the game of training. Since the leash is slack all of the time, and you've brought him to this point with few or no leash corrections, he is not heavily dependent on the leash. Abruptly taking the leash off would, however, invite him to learn a new game: finding out when you do or do not have control over him.

Instead, leave the leash on your dog, but you let go. Let him drag it as you practice heeling, stays, etc. You can quickly pick it up if your dog tries to take advantage of the situation (many never do). This applies to the long line as well. Let it drag on the ground. Practice recalls at first with the end of the line at your feet, dropping it just before you call your dog. When he is responding smoothly, don't worry about having the end near you when you call. Let your dog drag it behind him. Overcoming the drag of the line while coming when called and doing his other exercises will be good practice for him.

Continue to let your dog drag his leash or line as you work to polish the exercises. When you feel he responds just as well as when you held the end, begin shortening it. Use a shorter homemade line or have him drag the leash when he would have dragged the long line. Attach a short cord or "tab" for exercises you taught with the leash. Most likely your dog will keep working smoothly, but if he ever fails to respond, you can always reattach the longer line.

Many trainers leave a tab attached to their dog's collar, even when his response is flawless. If there is ever a need to restrain or move a dog unexpectedly, he will respond to the tab as he responds to a leash. Taking hold of a dog's collar invites resistance. It can be used in a pinch, but may upset training and is better avoided.

Integrating Training Into the Rest of Your Dog's Life

By now, you and your dog have accomplished a lot. His attentiveness and compliance have gradually improved, so that on your training walks you can get a prompt and willing response any time you call him, and on all of the other exercises, sit, stay, heel, and down.

He is not yet "trained." He has mastered a number of exercises in a familiar setting. If you want to take training to the next level, you will have to teach your dog to apply what he has learned beyond the context of your training walks. Dogs do not generalize as readily as people do; they "compartmentalize." They associate what they've learned with the particular situation in which they learned it, and can readily do the opposite in a circumstance that is only a little different.

It is normal for dogs to obey commands only for the person who taught them, for example. It is normal for them to do all of their obedience exercises at home, but go to obedience class and act as though they have no idea what you want. Even when trained inside the house, it is normal for dogs to act as though the rules don't apply when a visitor comes over. If you want your dog to generalize his learning to situations beyond his walks with you, it is up to you to help him.

In order to get your dog to respond to commands reliably in "real life," you must do three things.

1. **Vary the Setting.** Review and practice the obedience exercises in settings as close to real life as possible.

2. **Diversify the Rewards.** Incorporate a variety of real life rewards and consequences.
3. **Maintain Feedback.** Continue to acknowledge (praise) your dog's efforts and responses, and be prepared to follow through when he fails to respond properly.

Varying the Setting

It makes sense to review your dog's training in the settings in which you want him to respond. When he has practiced the right response in the setting where it is needed, he will truly understand what you expect.

New settings, or familiar settings where your dog is in the habit of thinking about things other than training, are distractions that make it difficult for him to concentrate. People struggle with distractions, too. I remember trying to answer a customer's training questions when my son was a baby. Someone was holding him so I could attend to the customer, but he was crying for me—and I was unable to put a single answer into words. Try to think of an analogous experience in your own life, so you understand the challenge your dog faces when you ask him to respond in the presence of distractions.

As you begin working around distractions, and whenever you begin training with new distractions or in a different setting, ask your dog only for the simplest of responses. You can require him to "sit" right by you, to "heel" for a very short distance, and to "stay" briefly with you close in front of him. Prompt him with patience and understanding if he fails to comply. You might need to review his obedience training from the beginning, perhaps taking several sessions before he can duplicate his best performances in this new environment.

A new setting is hugely distracting to the extent that your dog may not be able to respond at all. It is a good idea to prepare him by first working around minor distractions in a familiar setting, then more urgent distractions, incorporating elements that will be part of the new settings, before you begin asking him to respond in a completely different environment.

Simple distractions include anything new, such as a folding chair. More tempting distractions, which your dog will probably want to investigate, are people standing around, people talking, children playing, interesting scents (such as wildlife scents available at sporting goods stores), various items of food on plates, other animals, such as a tethered dog or a small animal in a cage, and an open gate or car door. If you use people as distractions, instruct them not to touch your dog or call his name. Calling your dog's name, remember, is a command for his attention, and will confuse the message that he is supposed to be ignoring them and attending to you. As for touching him, when you require your dog's undivided attention, you have a responsibility to protect him from the things he's now ignoring. If he is intruded upon or startled when attending closely to you, it will discourage him from concentrating in the future.

As always, work for a high proportion of success. You control your dog's success ratio by the level of difficulty of the exercises you ask him to do (distance from you on recalls and stays, length of stays and of heeling sessions between commands) and by the distance between your dog and the distraction.

When you have trained your dog around several different distractions and you introduce a new one, you may find that he is ready to ignore it and attend to you and your instructions. He is then ready to begin working in new settings. You can try generally distracting settings such as parks and shopping centers where there is plenty of noise, movement, and lots of people, or begin concentrating on places where you want good responses—in the house, at the veterinarian, or on the hiking trail.

A new setting potentially includes many individual distractions, plus the need to size up possible threats or social situations (canine or human) requiring a response. This is a lot for your dog to disregard. Be patient as you begin with the easiest of exercises, reviewing the sequence at a rate that maintains success. As he makes progress, feel free to concentrate on the commands you most expect to use in a given situation. Work on others as well, because collectively they convey the message that he is to pay attention and respond to you whatever happens.

Diversifying Rewards

You already use a small variety of rewards, sometimes acknowledging your dog's effort with a "good boy," petting him, practicing a well-known exercise, or occasionally giving him treats.

As you apply your dog's training to specific situations, you will make more use of rewards inherent to those situations.

Inside your house, you can use your dog's obedience to improve his citizenship and your ability to manage him. I strongly recommend using the sit-stay you have carefully taught. When you feed your dog, have him sit and wait as you set his food dish on the floor. Food is a strong temptation, so you may need to teach this in steps. After you stand up again, allow him to get up and eat with a release command. I advise continuing this throughout his life, relaxing it only if old age and arthritis make it difficult for him to sit.

Another situation where your dog's training to sit and stay is valuable is at any doorway. Instead of charging through doors the moment they are opened, or shouldering past you to impatiently nudge the door open, have your dog sit as you open the door, waiting for your release (whether or not you walk through the door first). You can probably see that this practice reduces the likelihood that your dog will knock someone down, or dart out the door and escape when someone comes in or goes out.

Your control of the everyday rewards of eating and going through doorways has other important benefits, too. Your dog is practicing self-control and, in waiting for your permission, he is acknowledging your leadership. This helps to uphold all of his training and helps prevent some of the behavior issues that can crop up in an unstructured, permissive home.

Practice the "down" and down-stay inside your home. It is

This dog is attentive as he waits for permission to go through the doorway.

useful to establish a place where your dog will go lie down on command. First practice down-stays in that spot, then begin telling him to "go lie down," and taking him to his place to lie down. Remember, as he stays for longer periods of times, to pay attention, putting him back if he gets up, and using a release command to let him know when it is OK to leave his place. Now you have a powerful tool to stop any unwanted behavior: require him to "go lie down." Because it is boring and involves social isolation, this is a mild punishment which, if used consistently, will act to reduce the frequency of most unwanted behavior.

You can also brush up recalls inside the home. Whenever

something is in store that you expect your dog will like, call him. Going for a walk, feeding him, giving him a treat, playing with him, brushing his teeth (if he has come to like that), anything that you know he likes. Don't waste these opportunities! On the other hand, if you think he will not like what you are about to do, for example if he dislikes having his nails trimmed, go and get him instead of calling.

Outside the home, the things most people want is for their dogs to come when called, and to be controllable around other people. Avoid the mistake of calling your dog when his fun is about to come to an end, whether he is playing with other dogs, exploring, or anything else he enjoys. Instead, when he has the opportunity to do something he particularly likes outdoors, first get him to do one or two obedience exercises before you release him to go play. Then, while he is playing, call him. Be prepared to go get him if necessary, but do not try to punish him in any way. Bring him to the place from which you originally called him, praise him, and let him go back to what he was doing.

With repetition your dog will learn that coming when you call does not mean an end to his fun, and he will come willingly—particularly if he knows you will come get him if he doesn't, and if once in awhile he gets an extra-good treat for coming. At the end of the day when it is time to go home, go and get him instead of calling.

You can train your dog to be as reliable as you desire in as many different settings as you choose. If you want him to respond immediately, everywhere, then practice to a high standard in a variety of places. Don't let there be any place that the rules do not apply. Be aware that different emotional states, including excitement, fear, and fatigue, act like extreme distractions. Ask for only the simplest, most basic responses under these conditions.

Maintaining Feedback

Think how nice it is when someone thanks you for something you have done; it recharges your motivation to do good things in the future. On the other hand, think of something you learned to do long ago that has never been enforced, such as precisely obeying every speed limit back in Driver Ed. It works the same way for your dog. If you apply his obedience in everyday life, acknowledging his efforts with "good dog" and making use of familiar rewards, remembering to use the "OK" release, and following through to prompt him if he fails, he'll continue to respond as you've taught him.

The nice thing about incorporating everyday rewards is that it's rewarding for us, too. I hope you will enjoy the communication with your dog, and his responsiveness, so much that it will be easy for you to continue the habit!

Opportunities for Further Training

If you have enjoyed training your dog, there are all kinds of opportunities to continue. You can showcase what the two of you have accomplished by entering an obedience match or trial. The American Kennel Club has opened its obedience events to mixed-breed dogs. This includes the newer sport of Rally Obedience, where dogs and owners apply their obedience skills while following directions through a course. Agility is a sport in which dogs learn to negotiate a variety of obstacles. In an event, a course of obstacles is set up. Handlers learn the course and then run it with their dogs, directing the dogs over and through the obstacles in the proper sequence.

You might want to train your dog to follow a trail and find lost objects in Tracking, or train for a sport specific to your breed. Hunting Tests, showcasing the traditional skills of hunting breeds, are available for retrievers, pointing dogs, and spaniels. Earthdog events give terriers and Dachshunds the opportunity to pursue their quarry through tunnels (the "quarry," caged rats, are not harmed in these events). Herding breeds can showcase their traditional skills in Herding Tests. Sighthounds can exercise their amazing speed in Lure Coursing events, and coonhounds can track and tree wild game in Nite Hunts. There are different venues of bite work (attack and protection training), Search and Rescue, Dock Jumping, and a competitive sport called Flyball.

Most dog sports offer multiple levels, including a level designed to welcome beginners. Other levels provide opportunities for motivated trainers and dogs to achieve more and more. Some sports include competition, and it can be intense. Others are pass-fail. A variety of ribbons and titles may be won.

Dock Dogs. This is photographer Stephanie Roberson-Thomas with her dog Sully.

The key to dog sports is the dog club. Clubs are made up of enthusiasts who put on organized events, and provide opportunities for their members to learn and train. Sometimes a club offers formal classes providing equipment and a training site; other clubs help members find compatible training partners for informal get-togethers.

If you are interested in learning about a particular dog sport, I recommend you start by attending an event or contacting a club. Events are normally licensed by a central organization. The American Kennel Club (AKC) licenses a wide variety of dog events. Through them you can find the dates and locations of events in your area, and contact information for the host clubs. The United Kennel Club (UKC) licenses obedience and hunting events, and the United States Dog Agility Association, North American Dog Agility Council, AKC and UKC all license agility events.

SHASTA

S hasta was my first dog. I trained him thoroughly in obedience. I planned to train my dog before I chose him or even settled on a breed. My research into dogs led me to read some of Vicki Hearne's moving stories about dog training. I knew I wanted my dog and me to have the kind of teamwork and communication she described.

My first idea was to adopt a dog from the local shelter, but as a renter without a fenced yard, I didn't meet their requirements. Thinking that a private breeder might be more flexible, I set out to visit breeders of a few dog breeds I thought would interest me. Dobermans were on the list, along with German shepherds and Labs.

I was still researching breeds when it happened. I was feeling a bit smug about the litters I'd viewed without getting carried away when I met a four-month old chocolate Lab. The breeder encouraged me to take him for a walk, and I fell like the proverbial ton of bricks.

I had a logical conversation with myself. I was finishing graduate school and not ready to care for a dog yet. On the other hand, though, the feeling I had for this dog might not be something to take for granted. I talked to the breeder, who agreed to keep the puppy for a reasonable boarding charge.

I visited my puppy a couple of times a week, and took him

for off-lead walks in the breeder's cow pasture. We avoided the cows, as the puppy was frightened by them, and I was none too comfortable with them myself. He swam in the pond, and learned to retrieve. I was so in love with this puppy, and hoped our activities would lead him to become attached to me.

One day I miscalculated, and we came face-to-face with a lone cow in a narrow passageway between larger fields. My puppy took one look and darted under the barbed-wire fence. I hoped that if I looked confident enough, the cow would let me pass without trouble. I straightened up and took a step forward. To my surprise, my puppy hurtled back through the fence, dashed up to the cow, and leaped away as she tried to toss him. He did this several times and, knowing that I couldn't stop him, I walked around the cow. As soon as I was safely away from the cow, my puppy came to join me.

It wasn't until afterward that I realized what had happened. My puppy had saved me from the big, mean cow. He was brave and wonderful and, best of all, he liked me. My puppy needed a name. I was sad that I would soon leave California, and wanted to give him a name that honored the natural beauty of his state of birth. I thought about Sierra, but settled upon Shasta after the spectacular, snow-capped mountain. I didn't anticipate that people would find this a not-very-masculine name. Oh, well.

As I approached the end of graduate school I had a more flexible schedule and was able to bring my puppy home. I enrolled in an obedience class. We were lucky to get a wonderful instructor. After the first lesson, that was for owners only, I came home and contemplated my puppy. What, I wondered, gave me the right to tell another being what to do and expect him to do it?

I went ahead with the class, telling myself that Shasta was going to be a big dog and had to be obedient. That was more of a rationalization than an answer to my question, though. In the years since I've become convinced that dogs are happier when they are trained. Understanding rules and having boundaries gives them confidence, develops communication with their owner, as well as a number of skills, and enriches their lives. I think that it's important to approach training with humility and respect for the dog. If there is a "right" to tell a dog what to do, we must earn it by being fair and diligent in our training efforts.

Shasta was the star of his obedience class, and a great companion through my last few difficult weeks of grad school. I walked him on leash through the neighborhoods, and off leash on the intramural playing fields, which were fenced and had none of the foxtail grasses that were said to be dangerous to dogs. I always carried appropriate supplies and cleaned up after him, of course.

One day Shasta and I were walking on the playing fields when an ambulance drove into the field. I noticed that a group of ballplayers were standing clustered together in the opposite corner, just as Shasta spotted something that interested him across the field. He took off on a path intersecting that of the accelerating ambulance, ignoring my calls.

The ambulance missed Shasta, but it opened my eyes to the difference between obedience class performance and real-life reliability. I set out to bridge that gap. I worked Shasta around all of the distractions I could think of, and then went out to practice in different settings. I remember practicing long sit-stays and down-stays where I was out of his sight. He became very reliable except that once in a while, he would ignore me when I called. Eventually I tried letting him drag a line around, enabling me to go get him if necessary, until coming when called was a way of life.

After graduating I drove across the country with Shasta to begin my new job in Washington, DC. I found a motel that allowed dogs in Elko, Nevada, and we camped the rest of the way. Shasta was a great traveling companion. Our only difficulty came when I needed to stop at rest stops in the heat of the day. I couldn't leave him in the car, but I could put him on a stay in the shade of a bush or tree while I went inside for a few minutes.

I continued taking obedience classes at our new home, teaching Shasta more skills and preparing to try obedience competition. Something kind of odd happened in these classes. The other students admired Shasta, but the instructors always seemed to find fault with us. Shasta had style. One day we were practicing coming-when-called one at a time. Our dogs started out on rubber matting, but the floor where we waited for them was linoleum. Shasta figured it out and, getting up some speed on the good footing, he sat early and slid up to me on the slick floor.

Another day we had a relay race, using the skills of sit-stay and coming when called. The class was divided into two teams. Each dog was supposed to sit and stay behind one line, while the owner walked away and stood behind another line about 30 feet away. Then the owner called the dog. If the dog got up before being called, the owner had to go back and sit the dog back down, and try again. If the dog stayed until the owner crossed the line, the owner called the dog, and when the dog crossed the farther line, the next owner could leave his or her dog.

My team decided Shasta should anchor the relay (run last). Halfway through it looked as though we might not get to go at all. My teammates were having to come back again and again to get their dogs to stay, and backing away from the dogs very slowly, so they wouldn't be tempted to follow. The other team was two dogs ahead of us. Sure enough, the other team's last dog was up while two dogs were still ahead of me. The last dog on the other team was a Golden retriever who did most things perfectly, but in slow motion. Remembering the dog's slowness, I encouraged my teammates not to give up. The Golden sat as his owner backed to the farther line, then slowly stood up when called.

The mixed breed that was third-to-last on my team took the scenic route but eventually got to his owner, while the Golden paced along. The person ahead of me commenced trying to get his wriggly Cocker spaniel to sit. He had to come back and re-sit her two or three times, finally backing away carefully. Fortunately the Cocker was quick to get to her owner when finally called. The instant she crossed the line I left Shasta at a run, having already told him to "stay." I knew he wasn't going anywhere. The Golden, moving steadily, had three or four feet to go. I called Shasta over my shoulder as I crossed the line. He dug out as if he understood this was a competition and it was close. He was still accelerating as he crossed the line inches ahead of the Golden. My team cheered. I felt Shasta had proved himself to even the most skeptical instructors.

I entered Shasta in Novice Obedience competition, and earned his Companion Dog title in three trials. Each time, Shasta and I were awarded a green Qualifying Ribbon and a red second-place-in-class ribbon. We also collected a bunch of special trophies for being the highest-scoring Labrador in the class and in the trial.

Shasta also passed a Therapy Dog test, which requires a dog to be under control and behave appropriately in challenging situations, and qualifies him to visit nursing homes and hospitals. We trained for the next level of obedience competition, Open, which includes jumping on command and retrieving. I had finally found people to help me learn retriever field work. I was eager to teach Shasta to do the work that was his breed's heritage.

The most important aspect of Shasta's obedience training was not the ribbons and titles he earned, but the degree to which he was able to be a part of my life. His training was especially useful when the unexpected happened. I was helping my cousin Mark move. We each drove trucks loaded with Mark's stuff. Shasta rode with Mark and my other Lab, Tahoe, rode with me. Mark pulled over at a toll plaza and got out of his truck to come talk to me (this was before mobile phones). Shasta followed Mark, jumping out the open window, but when I hollered, "sit!" he promptly sat by Mark's truck, out of the way of traffic.

Several years later, Shasta was riding with me when my pickup broke down. It was a very hot day, and I was pregnant. It would be dangerous to spend much time out in the heat. I waited for the tow truck inside a nearby bank. They would not allow Shasta inside no matter how well trained. I got Shasta some water, found a shady area in front of the bank and told him to lie down and stay. Shasta stayed. I watched from inside the bank as many passers-by stopped to pet him. He greeted them all with thumps of his tail, but never got up.

Shasta made me feel that I could train a dog, and the confidence he gave me was a big part of my decision to become a dog trainer. It wasn't until I had trained a lot of other dogs that I realized Shasta was exceptional. He was intelligent, cooperative, and forgiving of my mistakes. I have no doubt, though, as much potential as he had, Shasta would not have become quite such a wonderful, wise dog without the training that we did together.

CHAPTER 3

MANNERS

"Manners" refers to a dog's conduct around people, her owner and others. A well-mannered dog is pleasant and easy to be around. A dog with bad manners may have a lovable personality, but may require energy, effort, and tolerance from her owners. She may need to be kept away from children, older people, anyone wearing good clothes, and the dinner table.

Most people agree that good canine manners include keeping paws on the ground and taking care not to bump into people. Walking on lead without lunging or pulling is good manners. Responding to attention calmly is pleasant and polite. Some issues are a matter of owner preference. Begging for food is encouraged by some dog owners, and detested by others. Owners vary as to how they want their dogs to solicit attention. One might be flattered by being repeatedly nudged by his dog, while another might prefer her dog to lie at her feet and wait for attention.

The puppy section of this book suggests ways to develop good manners from the beginning. In this chapter we will focus on trying to change established bad manners and teach your dog to be more polite.

In order to change bad manners, it is helpful to understand how they develop in the first place. Bad manners are learned according to the same principles we use in training dogs. Circumstances may have induced the dog to respond in a particular way, and then repeated opportunities turned this response into a habit. Pulling while walking on leash is an example. Dogs have an automatic response to a steady pull on the leash: they pull against it. When an owner uses the leash to try to move a dog around, he or she induces the dog to pull, and the habit develops rapidly.

The action we consider "bad manners" may result in a reward for a dog. We may provide this reward unintentionally, or it may come from other people or the environment. A dog walking on a leash may, for example, suddenly lunge toward a tree. The person walking her is pulled off-balance and easily dragged a few feet. This is a popular trick among large dogs. Usually they know exactly how far they can drag their owners, and wait until they are within that distance of their destination to make a move.

This is a case of reward leading to repetition. The dog's first impulsive lunge was rewarded by unexpected progress and a chance to investigate the scents left at a tree. That initial success inspired the dog to try again. Repeated success quickly established a pattern.

Whether bad manners are induced and repeated, or if they gain a reward for the dog, they occur in a particular situation. The dog recognizes the situation by means of cues such as having a leash attached, being accompanied by her owner, the route of her daily walk and, in the second example, the sight of a tree. So in both cases, we need to teach the dog an alternative way to respond in that situation, identified by those cues. We are not telling the dog "do nothing," which would be very hard for her to understand. We are teaching her "do this other thing instead." Pulling and lunging will be replaced by an awareness of keeping slack in the leash.

We also need to find out what is inducing or rewarding the bad behavior, and put a stop to it. In the examples given, both involving problems walking on leash, we, the owners, need to stop pulling on the leash, and prevent ourselves from being pulled off balance (by being alert for the presence of trees and bracing ourselves).

One of the reasons many popular solutions for bad behavior does not work is that they don't do anything about the inducements and rewards that encourage the dog to keep doing the same thing. You may be advised, for example, to step on a dog's toes when she jumps up on you, or to knee her in the chest. Owners often find these measures to be ineffective. Their dogs keep jumping up. Jumping up is rewarding! There is probably an inherent reward of having completed a canine greeting ritual, plus an additional intermittent reward of attention, when we pet and talk to the jumping dog, forgetting that we

Your measures to discourage jumping won't work if you sometimes forget and reward jumping with attention.

are trying to improve her manners. Intermittent rewards are particularly effective at maintaining behavior. Consistency is emphasized in dog training because if you are not consistent in preventing a reward, your dog is getting intermittent rewards.

As you work to improve your dog's manners, be sympathetic to her point of view. Relearning, that is, overcoming an established habit, takes time and repetition. Plan to train consistently for a sustained period of time, and try not to get angry because she makes mistakes along the way. Young puppies are not so confirmed in their habits, so have less relearning to do. But they *are* puppies! Make allowances for your puppy's impulsiveness and playful nature. Have confidence that if you reward the right things, mannerly behavior will emerge as your puppy matures.

The overall plan for teaching good manners is to set up your dog's universe to induce and reward behavior you want, and to avoid inducing and rewarding actions you don't want. The rest of this section will be devoted to specific advice for teaching calmness, better leash manners, keeping paws on the floor, greeting people politely, walking around people without bumping them, soliciting attention politely, and refraining from begging.

General Calmness

For many dogs, the first step toward good manners is to calm down a bit. The dogs may wriggle, bounce, and seem unable to contain themselves when being petted, in the presence of people, or just in general. It can be hard to teach such a dog anything.

Roughhousing with your dog or encouraging her wildness with an excited tone of voice can induce wild behavior. Make sure if anyone in the household is getting your dog worked up, they stop. Paying attention to your dog when she is in a frenzy reinforces her excitement.

Attention is a powerful reward. It includes everything from looking at your dog, speaking to her, and petting her. You can use it to teach your dog calmness by giving her attention when she is calm, and withholding it when she is active or excited. If your dog loves to be touched, pet her gently when she is still. Withdraw your hands and look away when she wriggles or jumps. You do not need to withhold attention for a long time; as soon as she settles down, resume touching her. If your dog responds to your voice, you can use it in the same way.

Choose which behavior you want to reward. You will be amazed how quickly your dog learns the initial lesson of being calm. Be sure to follow up properly. Remember, your dog may be working against an established habit and will need time to form a new one. Keep on selectively rewarding calmness, making sure that others do not induce wild behavior, and your dog can change her ways.

Walking Without Pulling

A lot of dogs are hard to walk or control because they pull against the lead. They appear impatient with the pace of their walk, or perhaps eager to put distance between themselves and their struggling owners. I am convinced, however, that appearance is misleading, that they have simply learned to pull against the lead, and it has become habit. Like other issues we call "manners," leash-pulling is learned behavior. A taut lead, such as when we use the leash to pull them around, invokes an automatic resistance—the dog pulls in the opposite direction. Only a little repetition is needed to develop the habit of pulling against the restraint of the lead any time it is on the dog.

I have raised a number of puppies that never developed the habit of pulling. I believe the reason was that I avoided pulling on them. I expect this would work with many dogs, although possibly not sled dogs. The trick is never to pull on the puppy.

It takes concentration to care for a puppy or dog without ever pulling on her lead. Condition yourself to stop thinking of the lead as a means to move your dog around. Develop your skill at moving her by other means. Get her attention by saying her name, then use gestures and body language to encourage her to come to you, move over, etc.

The second part of the no-pulling strategy is to prevent or reduce instances where your dog might pull when you go for walks. When dogs frequently find their progress limited by the lead, they are more likely to put their heads down and pull against it. On the other hand, when reaching the end of the leash is a rare event, dogs are more inclined to back off or try going in a different direction.

The easiest way to reduce instances of tightening the leash is to use a longer leash. Then the area in which the lead is slack will be much larger. Your dog's natural tendency to move with you will contribute to keeping her within it most of the time. If you have access to a place where you can safely use a longer leash, I recommend it. You can use a longe line made for training horses, or make a long line from a length of rope and a bolt snap.

Don't use a retractable lead. The steady pull of a retractable lead is the effect we're trying to avoid. It doesn't matter, with most dogs, if they step over the line or even get it wrapped around their body. If yours is anxious about getting tangled,

Walking a dog on a longer line makes it easier to walk without pulling.

you may need to employ a bit of skill to keep her clear of the line, while preventing it from becoming taut.

Thus far we have eliminated the inducements to pull, and introduced your dog to an alternative of relaxing within a larger area. Because established habits can persist even without inducements or rewards, the solution to pulling has one more step. You will add a deterrent, a consequence to pulling that your dog would prefer to avoid. This will help her "wake up" from her habitual behavior and notice that you've made the alternative more appealing.

Dogs vary, and the severity of deterrent needed differs with the dog. Simply stopping any time the dog pulls works for most dogs. Their forward progress is interrupted, and they want to keep going. They will learn what they have to do to be able to walk uninterrupted. When your dog pulls, stop. Wait for her to stop pulling, by moving slightly toward you so that the leash slackens. As soon as it does, say "good," and start forward again.

Watch for signs that your dog recognizes this new consequence. If she pulls less frequently, or if she slackens the lead more quickly when it does tighten, she is learning to conform to your new rule. If you see either of these changes within three or four walks, simply stopping is an adequate deterrent.

If your dog shows no response, stop and call her to you any time she pulls. Instruct her to come all the way to you and sit before you praise her and begin moving forward again. This is a bigger interruption. Now she is required to transfer her attention to you and move away from anything she might have been eager to approach. Look for a decrease in frequency of pulling. Once your dog gets the idea, you may find it works just as well to stop and require her to take a step back toward you before continuing forward, or she may need the formality of coming all the way to you and sitting for a few seconds to keep her paying attention.

Remember that completely changing an established habit takes time. If your dog is showing signs of recognition, walking her should already be easier. Continue enforcing your new rule while she gradually replaces the old pulling habit with the new one of walking nicely.

There are a few dogs, typically young males from high-drive

working lines, who still do not get the message. They may anticipate being called in, and will bounce to your side when they feel the leash tighten, but as soon as they are released they are back out in front trying to drag you forward. These dogs need to be trained. They have a desire to make things happen, and it is better to channel this desire than to fight it. By training, you establish communication and respect. You might be surprised at the way your wild outlaw transforms into a willing, cooperative, and attentive worker. That is the nature of good working dogs. If you have this kind of dog, I recommend that you get in-person instruction from a trainer who has experience with high-drive working dogs.

In the interim, you may make some progress using physical corrections with a training aid, such as a properly fitted pinch

Dog wearing pinch collar.

collar. The pinch collar will tighten and become uncomfortable any time your dog starts to pull. A properly fitted pinch collar rides high on the dog's neck and has little or no slack in the chain portion. Adjusted this way, the collar will start to pinch the dog as soon as the lead tautens. If you are diligent in remembering not to haul your dog around, your dog will catch on quickly. Continue using the pinch collar for some time, as initial learning can be fast, but replacing old habits with new ones requires time and repetition.

If your dog has discovered the trick of pulling you off balance in order to drag you to a destination, such as a tree, you will have to anticipate her lunges and brace yourself so that they are never successful. This may be a tall order if your dog weighs nearly as much as you do. If she is overweight and throws her

Dog wearing a headcollar.

weight around, you will probably find that slimming her down brings about a miraculous improvement in manners.

If your dog is at a healthy weight, but is just large, strong, and determined, certain training aids can help you establish that you, not your dog, choose where you go, when, and how fast. There are several devices available that help give owners the edge with their big, strong dogs. Headcollars fit over the dog's head allowing you to attach the leash below your dog's muzzle, so that a pull on the leash turns her head toward you. Most dogs do not pull away when their heads are turned back toward the owner. On the down side, some dogs do not adapt well to wearing the headcollars, although a gradual introduction helps.

Harnesses are another option. The Easy Walk harness has a leash attachment in front of the dog's chest so that pulling will turn her body toward you. I have found it effective in controlling pulling with most dogs. Another type of harness tightens under a dog's "armpits" when she pulls. I have walked a few dogs with these; the dogs didn't pull and their owners credited the harness. In my experience, all of these devices become easier to use with practice. I would suggest buying them at a local pet-supply store with a good reputation, where someone will help you choose the right size and adjust it properly. Good shoes, or even cleats, will help you, too.

Removing the reward for lunging is only half of the solution. You also need to teach your dog an alternative. In this case, reward her for keeping the lead slack as you and she

Dog wearing Easy Walk harness.

approach a tree. If she refrains from lunging, turn and walk to the tree, giving her a chance to sniff and examine it as much as she wants. Once she recognizes the new rule, she will quickly learn to choose the option that gets her the reward of checking out the tree, or other interesting landmark.

You will have to remain aware of trees and other things your dog wants to investigate. You don't have to visit all of them, fortunately. Once your dog has the idea, checking out an occasional tree can be the intermittent reward that keeps her concentrating on mannerly walking, thinking that if she can just do well enough, you'll take her where she wants to go. Be sure to stop at different places on different days; unpredictability makes intermittent rewards effective.

Getting to sniff around a tree is this dog's reward for mannerly walking.

Staying Down

Another important area of manners is teaching your dog to greet people with her paws on the floor. As we want the dog to see it, "paws on the ground is a people magnet." This applies to sociable, outgoing dogs who seek to greet everyone they meet. In the absence of training to the contrary, they leap up towards a person's face, becoming more and more persistent as their leaping frequently nets them the attention they crave.

What are the inducements and rewards for jumping up? One of the reasons people struggle so much with jumping dogs is that there are strong inducements and strong rewards.

To understand the inducements, it is instructive to watch

Jumping up is easy to control with the right approach.

dogs interact with one another. Friendly dogs greet one another face to face, and often invite one another to play by jumping up and putting their paws on the other dog. Dogs are geared to seek face-to-face greetings, especially those who get to practice greeting other friendly dogs in the neighborhood, in day care, or at the dog park. Dogs don't automatically respond to human beings as if we were other dogs, but I think sometimes people approach dogs in a way that tells dogs that it's appropriate to treat us as if we were canine playmates. When we take an "aren't you cute!" attitude, speaking in an excited tone of voice, raising our hands, and even wriggling our bodies, it looks like an invitation to play.

The more sober among us aren't necessarily spared; a dog

who sees humans as playmates may conclude that reserved humans simply need a more vigorous invitation.

As for rewards, I suspect that if a dog completes the action of jumping, she feels intrinsically rewarded by having made an appropriate (she thinks) social overture. Sometimes people respond by putting their hands on a dog's shoulders and pushing her to the floor, which may be taken as a sought-after play response or as welcome attention. We may forget about consistency and training in our enthusiasm to greet our dog, lavishing her with attention in a direct reward for jumping up. It can be hard to remember when enjoying a dog, that they are always learning, so in effect we are always training. In addition, other people have the potential to confound our efforts, telling us "oh, I don't mind!"

It is possible to put a stop to all of these inducements and rewards! You will, however, have to temporarily isolate your dog from people who aren't sympathetic to your training efforts. Otherwise they will intermittently reward, and thus perpetuate, the behavior you are trying to change. Remain alert, and remember not to pet and cuddle your dog for jumping up.

Our retraining program will be to remove the inducements and the rewards for jumping up; to add a mild but effective punishment for jumping up; to set up one or more training situations in which your dog can learn that "staying down" earns rewards; and to practice "staying down" in an increasing variety of situations, up to and including former inducements such as strangers who wave their hands and talk baby talk.

After making plans to prevent uncontrolled encounters with people, the first thing you will do is to change how you respond when your dog jumps. Be prepared, and anticipate when she is likely to jump. Quickly (before she can make contact with you, if possible) take a step back. Assume a displeased expression and say "oh!" in an unhappy tone of voice. This makes her social overture a failure.

I find this "displeased reaction" is punishment enough where most dogs that come to me for training never jump on me a second time. These are dogs that have never met me before, so it's easy for them to learn my rules. If your dog has established the habit of jumping on people, you may need several repetitions. If you can get family members and other accomplices to react to your dog's jumping the same way you do, you may make rapid progress toward teaching her not to jump at all.

Many dogs need additional work, however. They need to know that keeping all four paws on the ground is good. To set up a simple situation in which your dog can learn the advantage of keeping her paws on the ground, it is helpful to have a barrier that she can see through, such as a baby gate or wire fence gate, or tether her to something. You can approach her, but she can't approach you. She will learn that she can get you to come to her by keeping her paws on the ground.

If your dog is an enthusiastic eater, incorporate a food reward into this exercise in a form that she will recognize and anticipate: her dish with her supper. If she is crazy for attention, you may not need the food. Approach, in her sight, from some distance away (at least a few steps, if you are inside the house).

This is a game that has simple rules. When your dog's paws are down, you approach her. Whenever her paws come up, you freeze. If she jumps and stays up, turn your head to one side, watching from the corner of your eye for her to drop back down. When she does, look directly at her and begin forward again. This setup allows you to respond instantly to your dog's actions many times, getting lots of repetition on the lesson, even though there is only one big payoff.

Opening the gate, when you finally get to it, may prove difficult. Keep on your toes, and if your touching the latch induces a jump, immediately withdraw your hand, taking a step back if that gets your dog down on the ground faster. Once you begin to open the gate, be prepared to slam it shut and step back if your dog jumps up. Usually, after a long approach in which they learn the beginnings of controlling their enthusiasm, dogs are less inclined to jump on a person than on a gate.

When you get to your dog and her paws are down, set down her supper or, if she is an attention hound, pet her and tell her she is a good girl. Quickly step back if she pops up in response to this attention. Repeat this once or twice a day. It can be a little frustrating at first, as the new concept your dog is learning—stay down to get the reward—battles with her long-standing expectation that she gets what she wants through action and effort, not to mention her inclination to express her joy at your approach.

You can teach sitting for supper in conjunction with the "paws down" lesson. I do it with all of the dogs that come for training, many of whom are outlaws their families can't control. At first, accept a brief "sit" on command, tell the dog "OK," and set down her food. At subsequent feedings, use the approach-and-retreat principle, lowering the pan as she sits, raising it up and reminding her to "sit" if she breaks. Pause and begin lowering again.

Accept a brief sit as you lower the pan partway, then try to lower it a little further at the next meal, and so on. Once the pan is on the floor, taking your hand away may provoke a break. If your dog does not wait for your "OK," snatch up the pan and straighten up, remind her to "sit," and try again.

Teach your dog to sit and wait for your release when you feed her.

Most dogs figure out that getting up early just delays their supper; a few are so excited by the prospect of food that they seem incapable of thinking. These dogs can benefit from lessons in self-control! Advance in small increments until she gets it.

Another game that teaches "keep paws down to get good things" can involve the whole family. Treats are a better choice for this lesson than attention, as petting or talking to your dog may seem like an invitation to jump. Tether her to a tree or stationary object. Family members stand around out of her reach and take turns giving her treats for staying down. The first person waits for your dog's paws to be down, steps forward, and starts giving her treats one at a time. It will be easier for her to succeed at first if you don't speak to her; as she catches on, you can challenge her more. The instant your dog starts to lift her paws off the ground, the person feeding her steps back out of reach. After she settles back down, the next person steps in and begins feeding her treats.

Whether you choose one of these exercises, or both, once your dog shows that she understands that keeping her paws on the ground draws people to her, you can begin to add challenges. Try speaking to her in a calm voice, while still making rewards dependent on her staying down. This lets her know that your voice is not an invitation to jump up. As she demonstrates that she understands, let your voice become more excited. When she resists jumping up in response to an excited voice, add enticing hand movements. Try to get someone new to join you and act exciting. Make sure the consequences are always the same, no matter what the distraction. Rewards are won by staying down.

Using these exercises your dog will soon grasp that staying down is a winning strategy, even when people seem to invite her to jump. The lesson will last longer, however, if you can wean her off of the food rewards. When she can resist jumping even if people talk in excited voices, you can begin using attention as a reward. Have everyone in the family make a point of lavishing attention on her when she stays down, and ignoring her when she even starts to jump.

Greeting visitors at the front door is still a temptation to jump. Arrange for one or more of the people who participated in her training exercises to come to the door. When you open it,

Reward your dog with attention for standing politely on the ground.

they should back away in dismay if your dog jumps, but come in and greet and pet her if she stays down. If you can find a new accomplice to repeat this routine, your dog will get the message that staying down is the answer, no matter who shows up at the door, regardless of how excited you sound when you greet them.

Care Around People

In addition to walking without pulling and greeting people politely, dogs with good manners should show an awareness of people's legs and not barge into them. A medium-sized dog can knock down a child or older person, and anyone can fall over a dog when carrying something bulky, especially if they don't see her.

My strategy for teaching dogs to be careful around people's legs is simple: if they bump me, I yell at them. Punishment is appropriate here because we really want the dog to be on the lookout for the possibility of contacting someone's legs, and to try to avoid it. One of the rules for effective punishment is that it must be used sparingly. If you do not yell at your dog for anything else, she will take notice when you do it. Sound angry. I do a lot of work with Labradors, many of whom have developed enthusiasm for body-slamming their playmates. It usually only takes one or two instances of being shouted at for them to carefully avoid bumping people.

As always, be careful that you are not encouraging the behavior that you want to eliminate. If you or anyone else pets your dog and pays attention to her as she stands between their legs, she will learn to push her way between people's legs in search of attention. If she does, she risks knocking people down. Make sure everyone who is encouraging this dangerous behavior stops, and get everyone to try to stand with their feet together so she doesn't have the opportunity. As time goes by without opportunities to dart between people's legs, she will gradually lose the habit.

Attention Seeking

Some of the things dogs do in pursuit of attention can be offensive. They may shove their heads into people's laps, bark, mouth their owners' hands, or even bite. We inadvertently teach dogs these strategies by getting absorbed in other things, and ignoring the dogs until they do something too obnoxious to disregard. Then we reward them with attention.

To remove the reward, change the dynamic. If your dog is at large, be aware of her need for attention, and respond to her before she gets obnoxious. If you must concentrate on something, and cannot keep track of your dog's behavior, confine her in a safe place so that she can't pester you.

Decide what is an acceptable way for your dog to seek your attention. This is an opportunity to make use of any training you have done. She wants attention, so she is primed to respond to a command. Do you want her to sit politely, offer a paw, or lie down? When you can see her getting restless, before she starts the obnoxious behavior, give her a command, and reward her with attention when she does it. Dogs tend to the more efficient; soon, instead of trying other behaviors first, yours will start out with the one she knows will win your attention.

Begging, and How to Make it Work for You

Begging for food is considered acceptable by some dog owners, and bad manners by others. If you think it's cute when your dog begs, there's no need to do anything about it, unless you would enjoy teaching her to do tricks. A begging dog is training herself to earn treats by composing her face for maximum sympathy, and inventing cute wriggles and vocalizations to go along with it. You can take advantage of this ready-made training opportunity to shape the begging into any number of tricks. You can get your dog to sit up, roll over, high-five, or anything else you can think of. It's simple. Withhold the tidbit until she makes some move toward the action you have in mind. Say "yes!" at the exact moment she does it, then give her a treat.

If you want to train her to sit up to beg, for example, you might wait for her to make some upward movement, perhaps stretching her head a little higher than usual, then say "yes!" If you want to teach her to high-five, you have to first get a paw off the floor. Watch for her to lift a front paw slightly, or even just to shift her weight off one paw. Your well-timed "yes!" tells your dog exactly what she did to earn her reward.

When you repeatedly reward an action, your dog will do it more and more. You can start choosing only the best efforts,

High-five.

gradually shaping her response into the action you have in mind. This kind of training can be a lot of fun, and impresses people. It is the approach used in clicker training, by the way. Your dog experiments to find out what action causes the sound ("yes!") that tells her a reward is coming. This is a good opportunity to learn this style of training, as your dog's motivation and willingness to experiment are already established.

If you don't want your dog to beg, then step one is to eliminate the reward. Identify everyone who is feeding your dog from the table, and convince them to stop. Next, discourage begging with a little mild isolation. Once you have taught your dog to lie down and stay, you can tell her "go lie down." Guide her across the room to a spot where she will be safely out of the way, make her lie down, and tell her to "stay." Remember to let her up at the end of the meal. "Go lie down" can also be used for obnoxious attention seeking when you slip up and fail to notice the early signs. It is also useful when you have a guest who does not want to be approached by your dog.

If you don't want your dog to beg but think it would be fun to teach her tricks, there's a solution for you, too. Use her begging to teach her a trick. Give the trick a name, like "high-five," and say the name every time she does it. Now establish a new rule: she doesn't get anything for offering you a high-five unless you have said, "high-five." Once she learns this rule, you are in control. You can get her to do her trick on command, and desist the rest of the time.

If you don't like your dog's manners, take heart. Most of the behavior we think of as "manners" is learned, and your dog can learn to behave differently. For most issues of manners, a two-part strategy is best. Replacing an unwanted behavior first requires finding out how it is maintained. Something or someone is inducing the behavior, rewarding it, or both. This must stop if your dog is to stop the behavior. And it must stop consistently, because an occasional or intermittent reward is like hitting the jackpot in a casino—your dog will try again and again just in case this attempt will be successful.

The second part of replacing bad manners is to teach your dog an acceptable alternative, because "do nothing" is a difficult assignment, and if she has to make something up you may not like it.

Set up your dog's universe to reward the behavior you want, and consistently avoid rewarding the behavior you don't want.

Walking nicely on leash and greeting people politely are common dog owner concerns. In both cases, understanding a bit of canine nature, their reaction to a steady pull and the social context of jumping, helps us find effective strategies to fix bad manners. Begging is an interesting problem; many dog owners despise it, but it provides an opportunity to experiment with a creative and elegant training technique.

Remember to exercise patience when retraining your dog. Recognition of the new rules usually comes quickly, but plenty of time and repetition are needed to completely change an old habit.

SMOKY

Smoky was the most amazing puppy. Maybe I shouldn't have been surprised, because I had trained several dogs from his bloodlines and they were all cooperative, smart, and easy to train. This was the reason I wanted a puppy from that litter. I didn't worry about which puppy; in fact I had the second-last pick. The breeder chose, and sent Smoky to me.

Smoky, like his older relatives, was agreeable and pleasant to be around. He was cooperative, retrieving to hand when most puppies would experiment with running off, and readily learning everything I tried to teach him. What amazed me most about Smoky, though, was that he never once pulled on the leash, from the first time I put it on him. Like many owners, I have struggled with big, strong, pulling dogs. It used to take me a lot of work to teach them to walk nicely on leash. The draft-horse tendency seemed to be built in; yet here was a puppy who didn't do it.

Smoky was pretty good about learning not to bite hands. There was only one thing he did that was a problem. When we were walking, he would attack my legs, leaping up and biting. He put holes in a couple of my pairs of jeans, and in my legs, too. His teeth would get caught in the fabric, and I was surprised that he never broke a tooth. I was somewhat surprised that the wrenching his mouth got as I walked didn't discourage these attacks—I guess they were enough fun for him to be worth any discomfort.

With time, effort, and maturity, Smoky learned not to jump and bite. I can't remember what approach I used to discourage him, just that I had to work at it.

I had bought Smoky with the plan to train him for retriever field trials, which are extremely competitive, so his training to retrieve began right away. As a puppy, he was an eager retriever, focused on getting his object, undaunted by water, brush, or any other obstacle. He learned all of his obedience commands quickly, and when it was time to learn formal fetching and delivery, that was easy, too. I taught Smoky the basics of a blind retrieve, where he would go in the direction I pointed him for a retrieve he hadn't seen. When I blew a whistle, he would stop, turn, sit, and look at me for a hand signal to tell him what direction to go. Smoky learned all of this with ease.

Once these nuts and bolts were mastered, I turned Smoky's training over to my husband, John. At that time, I was training young dogs, and John would take them over and develop their skills in the field. At first John was enthusiastic about Smoky, but before long he started having problems. Smoky was cooperative and courageous, but when he got farther than about 150 yards away, he wasn't taking directions. I couldn't believe it, but came out to watch John work Smoky. Sure enough, beyond about 150 yards, Smoky almost never took his handles correctly. He was having trouble with marked retrieves, where he got to watch the dummy fall, at longer distances, too.

I wondered if Smoky was nearsighted, and John and I set up some experiments to test his vision. Sure enough, it looked as though Smoky just couldn't see well enough to do the things we wanted him to do.

My Dad, around that time, had an eight-year-old German Shepherd. Dad had struggled with that dog, who was a car-chaser and pulled so badly on leash that he could hardly walk him. I suspected Dad might have gotten into some dangerous situations with his unruly car-chasing dog. I felt bad for Dad, having such a difficult dog, and had long thought a Lab would be a better dog for him. Dad's dog died around the time John and I discovered Smoky's nearsightedness.

I asked my Dad if he'd like to have Smoky. I think Dad was happy to skip the puppy stage and get a dog that already had training, and manners, especially a dog that would walk without pulling. Dad came to visit and took Smoky for several walks. He was astounded and delighted that a dog could walk without pulling. He took Smoky home with him.

Dad had an amazing dog who would never pull, and Smoky had an owner who would give him more attention than John and I ever could, and throw retrieves for him at a distance he could easily see. Everyone, I figured, could now live happily ever after. Except there was a wrinkle.

A few months later I was talking with my Dad, and was asking him questions, and found out that, of all things, Smoky was now pulling when Dad walked him! I was astounded, and chagrined that the dog I had given Dad didn't live up to the billing I had given him. Not being on the spot to see what was going on, I encouraged my Dad to get help from a local dog trainer. He did, and I heard snippets about the interaction with the trainer. The trainer had advised a change of food, and told my Dad that Smoky was trying to be "dominant." Dad had to do all kinds of things to stop Smoky from being dominant, like making sure he went through doors ahead of the dog, and other symbolic gestures.

That didn't sound like the Smoky I knew, but I never expected him to start pulling, and I wasn't there to observe. I did notice, however, that the next couple of puppies I raised also learned to walk without ever pulling on the leash. Smoky was no longer the only dog I'd raised who never pulled; he was merely the first. Interesting. Maybe it wasn't Smoky who was different; maybe what I was doing with puppies was different than in the past.

I figured it out. Smoky and the other puppies learned to walk without pulling because I never pulled on them. Smoky started pulling for my Dad because, like many dog owners, Dad pulled on Smoky. I'm not sure how well the training lessons turned out. I know Smoky continued to pull, because eventually I went to visit and walked him. It wasn't so bad that Dad couldn't walk him, though, and the two of them went for walks together religiously twice a day.

I saw no justification for the notion that Smoky was "dominant." He was still a cooperative dog, just one who happened to be in the habit of pulling. I think there is merit to the idea of teaching a dog to be under control at doorways. I don't think it matters who goes through the door first. I think the issue is that when the door opens, the dog is attentive to his owner, and exercising self-discipline, rather than charging through heedlessly.

Smoky died earlier this year. He provided my Dad many years of companionship. He taught me an important lesson about how dogs learn to pull, and about manners in general. We teach dogs to pull by pulling on them. Other bad manners are learned somehow, and finding the circumstances that perpetuate them is the first step to changing them.

Despite not having been quite as inspired in his understanding of manners as I once thought, Smoky was an exceptional dog of great courage and character. I miss him, as I know Dad does, and I feel privileged to have known him.

CHAPTER 4

SOLVING BEHAVIOR PROBLEMS

Sometimes dog ownership goes smoothly, but frequently it involves wrinkles in the form of undesirable behavior. In keeping with the general approach of this book, we will treat the problems that arise *as behavior*, as something that your dog has learned to do, subject to forces in his environment. Behavior can be discouraged, replaced by other (acceptable) behavior, or prevented until your dog has forgotten about it. There is no need to postulate that your dog is intentionally "defying" you, or plotting to take over the household. Instead, learn to analyze your dog's behavior. See what features of his environment are reinforcing, or supporting, the behavior, and use the strategies in this section to teach him a new way to behave.

Try to approach the misbehaving dog with sympathy. He has misunderstood what is acceptable behavior, or perhaps he is reacting to something in the environment of which you are unaware. This can be hard for owners who feel they've made their wishes clear, but dogs don't read our minds as well as we often assume; they get the message only when we make the rules and the consequences obvious.

Historic dog trainer Bill Koehler said that in addressing dog behavior problems, "a big patch makes the best mend." If you socialize and train your dog, teach him manners, and enforce sensible rules around the house, problems will be fewer and more tractable than they will if you have little input into his life except to react to problems when they occur.

If you have turned to this section first, then here's a plug for the other sections of the book. To "fix" behavior problems, you can attach consequences to your dog's behavior that influence him to behave differently. But you will have many more strategies available, understand your dog better, and your dog will be much better attuned to your efforts, if you teach the basic obedience commands. Work on teaching him to seek what he wants through good manners, rather than through a pell-mell disregard of those around him.

One of the reasons that owners struggle with their dogs' behavior is that much of the popular advice on the subject is counterproductive. To be blunt, at best the most common advice causes owners to neglect effective options for improving their dogs' behavior. Frequently, however, tactics like punishments and "alpha" strategies harm owner-dog relationships, create new problems, and make existing problems worse.

Because these bad ideas are so heavily promoted, I will debunk them briefly before moving on to strategies that can actually help. Effective strategies include obedience training, preventing opportunities to engage in problem behavior, distracting your dog and redirecting his attention to an appropriate activity, training an incompatible behavior, desensitization and counterconditioning, and identifying and fixing the causes of problem behavior.

After describing these proven techniques, I'll discuss the common, often misunderstood problem of aggression. I strongly recommend in-person help from an expert in dealing with aggression. The discussion here is intended as general background to illustrate that aggression is not all mysterious and unpredictable. Frequently there is a definitive solution.

Please remember, in making decisions regarding your dog, to be appropriately skeptical. Just because you hear something frequently, or see it in print or on TV, does not mean it's right. I speak as someone who's been in print and on TV.

Many dog owners assume punishment is the right way to deal with behavior problems. Most of the time it fails, but owners go on punishing their dogs. Their unshakeable belief in punishment prevents them from seeing that it isn't working. Punishment does work, for some things, in some situations, if applied just right. If it works, it will be obvious, as it only takes one or two applications. Please remember this. If you must punish your dog, recognize that a punishment that doesn't get results by the second application is ineffective, and stop.

Punishment frequently has unintended effects, causing a variety of fears and inhibitions that can be worse than the original problem. Some dogs are sensitive and any harsh treatment overwhelms them, dominating their view of their world, and their owner. This includes shouting; many dogs show considerable distress when shouted at.

Later in the chapter I'll review some of the "rules" for effective punishment. I hope if readers understand the limitations of its effectiveness, as well as some of its pitfalls, they will choose alternative, more effective means to change problem behavior. One of these rules is that punishment only works if it is used sparingly, so it is essential to find alternatives to punishment in most situations.

Thinking that we must use "alpha theory" in order to prevent our dogs from taking over and becoming monsters is the next most damaging popular suggestion. This series of suppositions strung together has no value for the dog owner, but can lead to paranoia, antagonism, and repeated punishment of the dog. Negative attitudes and unpredictable punishments harm a dogs' trust in their owners as well.

Dogs do seem to respond well to good leadership. Owners can assume a leadership role by being fair, establishing clear rules, and controlling their dog's access to "resources," which are things the dog values, including food, treats, toys, outings, and play opportunities. The approaches described in this book to training, puppy raising, and developing manners promote this style of ownership.

Exercise and "neutering" are two more ineffective strategies commonly proposed to address all kinds of behavior issues. Dogs can become destructive and/or challenging if they do not get enough physical and mental stimulation or challenge. Exercise alone rarely changes this; it just creates a fitter dog with a greater need for exercise and stimulation. An increase in quality attention, such as training, is a better solution. In some cases a second dog will fulfill these needs; but owners need to consider carefully if they want the additional responsibility.

"Neutering" of male dogs has long been recommended as a panacea for almost everything, with little justification. Thanks to James Sirpell and colleagues at the University of Pennsylvania, we finally have definitive information on this subject. Neutered males, as a group, display a greater incidence of all kinds of behavior problems than do intact males. Many veterinarians are still unaware of this research, and of the recent findings that neutering appears to increase the incidence of orthopedic problems including hip dysplasia, certain deadly cancers, and canine cognitive dysfunction.

As a dog owner you are responsible for your dog's reproductive potential. Whether you choose to control it through "neutering" or some other means is up to you. Do not expect, however, that the procedure will solve any behavior problems. Plan to address these through training and management.

Punishment, pretending to be an alpha wolf, exercise, and surgery won't resolve your dog's behavior problems. Fortunately there are a number of effective strategies you can use. The techniques described here provide an array of tools for addressing all kinds of problems, including stealing, destructive behavior, and problems related to fear.

The Manners section gives detailed instructions for dealing with the common issues of pulling on leash, jumping up, crashing into people, and begging at the table. Most of those problems respond to a two-part approach. First, figure out what is encouraging the behavior and put a stop to it. Then, teach the dog a different, better way to behave in the same situation.

This section focuses on the strategies for changing behavior. Once you appreciate how they work, you can use them to solve a wide array of problems. Training an incompatible behavior, used repeatedly in the Manners section, is among them.

Strategies to Change Problem Behavior

Prevent Opportunities and Control Privileges.
Unwanted behavior really does go away by means other than punishment. The simplest way to get rid of it is to prevent opportunities. Behavior that is never practiced and rewarded will fade away and disappear.

Prevention of opportunities is a continuation of the recommendation from the puppy-raising section, to confine your dog to a place where he cannot get into trouble any time you aren't able to supervise him, and to supervise him and guide his behavior any time he isn't confined. Preventing opportunities works in multiple ways. First, it immediately stops damage caused by your dog. Second, much behavior, if not practiced, will eventually disappear. This is particularly true if you can catch it early, before it's become an established habit. If your dog digs, don't leave him unattended in the yard. If he steals food from the kitchen counter, don't let him in the kitchen unless someone is there to pay attention to him and stop him from doing so (having him wear a leash that you can quickly step on will help). If the problem has become established as habit, you will also need to train your dog to do something else when the opportunity to misbehave presents itself. More on this later.

There's a deeper benefit to preventing opportunities. In order to prevent opportunities, you may restrict your dog's freedom, controlling access to some of his or her privileges. He will not be able to do just what he wants, whenever he wants to do it, but will be dependent on you. You will be the key to everything he wants in life: food, treats, outings, play opportunities, time with the family, etc.

Do not shirk this role. More than anything else you can do, it will cause your dog to view you as a leader. Go a tiny bit farther and require a particular response (be fair—ask for something you have taught your dog to do) prior to all of your dog's pleasures, and you will soon find you have a lot more control over his or her behavior. You establish a simple logic: your dog gives you what you ask in order to get what he wants. He will look to you for opportunities to earn privileges.

This is control. You do not rigidly control your dog's behavior; you control his access to all pleasures, and you control the environment in which he learns how to behave. Dog trainers refer to this approach as "Nothing In Life Is Free," or NILIF.

It is widely recommended for resolving a variety of problems, including out-of-control, demanding dogs and some cases of aggression. Detailed, structured NILIF programs are available for owners of these extreme cases to follow. By incorporating the basics into your life with your dog from the beginning, you can prevent that kind of trouble, and solve minor problems easily.

What are some ways you can prevent opportunities to practice bad behavior, and control privileges? I already mentioned using a leash to control your dog's misdeeds in the kitchen. There's no reason your dog can't wear a leash in the house. You can keep him in sight, and have the means at your fingertips to stop him from stealing, chewing, soiling the house, harassing

There's no reason your dog can't wear a leash in the house.

other pets, you name it. You do not have to keep him tight on a short leash, as long as you can get to him and stop him before the bad behavior gets under way.

Going outside is a privilege. Ask your dog to sit politely before you open the door. Work up to getting him to sit still as you open the door, remaining in place when it is wide open, getting up and running outside only when you say "OK!" Hint: start modest, increase your requirements slowly, and be prepared to quickly shut the door, or step on your dog's leash, if he gets up without permission.

Eating is a privilege. Teach your dog to sit and wait for your release as you set down his food bowl. If you want to, you can hand feed him, requiring him to sit politely at each handful and to take the food gently from your hand (close your hand if he is rough or careless).

Playing with other dogs, if it is something your dog likes to do, is a privilege. He will probably be pretty motivated, and you can capitalize on this to get him to do a little obedience routine comprising several commands, perhaps a recall, sit, finish to heel, and stay as you walk away and return. At first he will be impatient, so don't ask for too much right away. Build up his routine over several days. You can further establish control by practicing recalls during his play session. Let him play with a line attached so you can go get him if he doesn't come, which is likely to happen at first. When you call him, if he comes, sit him, praise him, and let him go back to play. If he doesn't come, go get him, bring him to the place where you called, then sit him, praise him, and let him go back to play. This will teach him that coming doesn't necessarily mean an end to his fun. As his responses get better, you can add a penalty for failing to come: you go get him but don't let him go back to play. The game is over.

If your dog likes to chew, then a chance to gnaw on a prized chew toy is a privilege (be sure to choose toys that are safe for your type of dog). Give him access to a favorite chew toy as long as he stays in an assigned place, such as on a mat, in a corner of the kitchen, or in a crate with the door open.

A crate or other safe place to confine your dog is an important adjunct to preventing opportunities and controlling privileges. Uncontrolled access to trouble and fun will erase any gains you try to make, and will teach your dog that your control has limits, and the absence of his leash is the cue to go wild.

Loss of Access

This technique works in situations where your dog has access to something he wants, and is engaging in behavior you want to correct. The moment he begins misbehaving, cut off his access. He may be enjoying attention from a visitor, for example, and decide to start sniffing where it is unwelcome. You can arrange things so that his choice costs him the attention he has been enjoying. Don't make a flying grab for your dog, as that will signal that you are not in control of the situation. Instead, just have your visitor immediately stop petting him. A few repeats of this may do the trick, or you may want to set him up for a lesson. The clearest way to make this point is for the offended person to promptly step out of your dog's reach, and stop petting and/or talking to him. You will have to enlist the help of a friend ahead of time, and have a leash on your dog so that your friend can step out of reach.

The Manners section describes a similar approach as part of a strategy to teach your dog not to jump up on people.

Loss of access is a form of punishment, called "negative punishment" by trainers because it involves taking something away, in this case privileges. Like more familiar forms of punishment, it works only when it is not overused. Your dog must have a chance to enjoy his privileges in order to know what he's losing, and if they are taken away for a variety of unrelated infractions, he may never get the picture. To make sure your dog gets a clear message, identify one behavior for which loss of access is most appropriate, and then apply it consistently.

Loss of access works well for minor problems inside the home. Begging at the dinner table can be treated by putting your dog on a long down-stay on the other side of the room. An outburst of rambunctiousness or sudden bad manners could lead to confinement in a crate or safe room. The loss-of-access concept is also used by experts in treating some forms of aggression, although that is beyond the scope of this book.

Interrupt and Redirect
Interrupting a problem behavior, "before it gets off the ground," can be very effective. Of course a dog with nothing else to

do may try again the next moment. To prevent this, we usually accompany an interruption with a "redirection" to some other activity. Frequently we praise or reward the dog's change of focus. Repeated applications will often result in the dog's initiating the second, acceptable activity in the circumstances where he might otherwise have tried the unwanted behavior.

Interruption and redirection are effective in many situations where punishment has been the traditional choice. It appears that what is needed is not so much to discourage the dog as to turn his attention to a different, and potentially rewarding, activity.

Corrections in training are an example of interruption and redirection. Praise or reward upon completion of the redirected behavior makes that choice more likely in the future. In the obedience section, for example, I describe what to do when your dog gets out of position. You move so as to exaggerate his error, give a quick tug and verbal "ah!" to get his attention, and prompt him with the leash to return to your side. Finally, you praise warmly as he returns to correct position and gives you his attention.

Dogs tend to streamline, to adjust their behavior to be more efficient. In other words, they learn to "cut corners." With repetition they will drop the initiation of the bad behavior, and go straight to the action that gets rewarded.

Interruption and redirection are useful in house-training. Most puppies and dogs make a "mistake" at some point, beginning to relieve themselves in the house. This is another instance where punishment is not only unnecessary, but likely to make things worse. Interrupting the dog, as early as possible so that the need for relief is still present, is a better option. Bearing down on him while talking in a cheerful sing-song will usually stop what he is doing without frightening him. Then the dog is whisked outside to his established spot. It can take awhile for him to get over the excitement and finish relieving himself, but when he does, he gets praised.

The "wrong" behavior, i.e. relieving himself in the house, was never completed. Instead, the dog relieved himself in the correct spot and was praised for it. These are the necessary elements for him to learn; punishment would add nothing except possible problems. Some dogs that are punished during house-training, for example, learn to avoid relieving themselves in their owner's presence. This can start a vicious cycle, where the owner cannot get the dog to "air" outside, and then after the owner departs the dog relieves himself in privacy—in the house.

With vigilance, chewing can be redirected to some degree. Interrupt your dog any time he begins to lick or look interested in chewing something valuable, and get him settled with an approved chew toy. It helps to have a variety of appealing chew toys available. To help your dog make good choices, don't give him anything like old shoes, which are a lot like new shoes, as chew toys.

Many dogs learn to chew only appropriate objects with a little guidance. Some dogs are more difficult, or subject to "for-

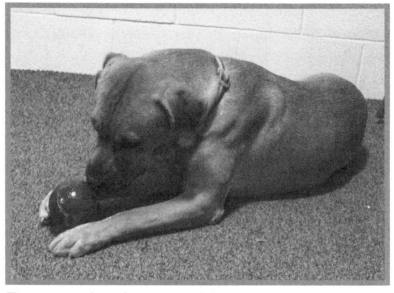

Encourage your dog to chew on approved chew toys.

getting" and chewing up their bed, or a few shoes, after seeming reliable for months. Retrievers seem prone to this.

Destructive outdoor behavior such as digging and stripping the leaves off small trees can be controlled by interruption and redirection, but it takes time and attention. A dog who is left outside alone with opportunities to dig and destroy will probably do considerable damage, have a lot of fun, and develop bad habits.

A diligent owner can convince his or her dog that certain activities are "non-starters," using primarily interruption and redirection. If you are practicing control over access and have a leash or other ready means to promptly interrupt your dog, you can be very effective at teaching him to behave.

Train an Incompatible Behavior

Your dog can't do whatever it is you don't want him to do if he is busy doing something else instead. Training an incompatible behavior means teaching your dog to favor doing something else in the situation where he would previously misbehave, preferably something so different that it leaves no room for the unwanted behavior. Interruption and redirection is an example of teaching an incompatible behavior. Sometimes it takes a little more ingenuity to replace one behavior with another.

Many behavior problems occur only in a particular context, such as barking when someone comes to the door, or urinating in the house when his bladder is full and he can't hold it any more. There are signs associated with the context, or "cues," that have come to be triggers for the undesirable behavior.

To replace misbehavior with an acceptable alternative, first teach the wanted behavior as an exercise, using rewards. Identify the cues that trigger the problem behavior. Now, teach your dog to do the new exercise in response to the cues you have identified. Suppose, for example, that your dog barks when someone comes to the door, and your regard the barking as a problem. Perhaps he goes on and on, works himself into a frenzy, and leaps against the door. Or maybe he acts aggressive toward visitors when the door is opened.

First, you need to choose a good alternative behavior that is incompatible with barking at the door. You could teach your dog to go to a predetermined spot and lie down there, or you could teach him to come to you. Coming to you gives you the chance to immediately acknowledge and reward his good choice, increasing the likelihood he'll make the same decision again. Once you have taught your dog to come when called, as described in the Obedience section of this book, practice recalls in the house. Practice calling your dog to all of the places where you usually spend time, and from all of the areas he usually spends time. If he responds by following you around the house, you can use the "stay" command to get far enough away to call him. All of this obedience is excellent practice, by the way, that will tend to improve all aspects of your relationship.

Once your dog is responding well all over the house, put him on a sit-stay and have a helper knock on the door (or ring the doorbell). Immediately call your dog. Set him up for success on this by making the recall very easy, with both of you in the same room a few feet apart. If you anticipate that your dog will not obey when he hears someone at the door, prepare by having a cord on him. Reel him in if necessary, sit him under control, and give him his reward.

Continue to practice until your dog comes successfully when you are in the same room. Then begin working in different places around the house, as before, but with the added challenge of the knock on the door (or doorbell). You can add a variation. When your dog comes to you, praise him and say, "let's go see who it is." Have him walk with you under control to the door, open it, and have your accomplice give him a treat. If your dog breaks away and runs to the door without you, all you have to do is not open it. If he comes to get you and walks politely, go to the door, open it, and he gets his treat. If on the way to the door your dog gives in to excitement and charges ahead, just stop and wait for him to return to you. You control the door, and your dog wants the door to open. He is capable of learning to follow your rules in order to get you to open it.

You can extend the rules to require your dog to greet the visitor politely. Because he anticipates a reward, your dog is likely to pay close attention to what it takes to get the reward. If your assistant turns his or her back and withholds the treat in response to being jumped on, then gives the treat when your dog is standing on all fours, your dog should quickly learn to stay down. If your dog is so committed to jumping that he doesn't get the message, check the Manners section for additional exercises to teach "stay down." Most dogs will fine-tune their behavior to suit your whim once they understand that you control the door, and the treats.

If visitors come by and you hurry to answer the door, forgetting all about your training program, your dog is likely to get rewarded for the wrong thing—charging the door and barking. Rewarding unwanted behavior will undermine your training, so try to prevent this during the time you are retraining him. If you know when someone is coming over, put your dog in a crate or other safe place. If someone drops in and your dog charges the door, do not open it. Explain through the door that you must put your dog up, and do so before opening the door.

Some owners prefer to let their dogs bark for a few moments until told "thank you" or "that's enough." You could teach that much the same way, just delay calling your dog until he's had a chance to bark briefly. Either way, a side effect to this training is that your dog will look more to you as the person who controls what goes on in the house, rather than thinking it is incumbent upon him to announce visitors, defend the house, or whatever he feels his responsibility is.

What about the dog that urinates in the house if he is left in too long, or else paws and scratches at the door? He can be taught an alternative. It is not altogether incompatible, but he will like it better as will you. Teach him to ring a bell to tell you when he needs to go out.

This is a useful and relatively easy trick. Most people use several jingle bells on a ribbon or piece of fabric. Hang them from the doorknob of the door you use to let your dog outside to relieve himself, so that part of the ribbon/fabric is at nose height. Ring the bells every time you open the door for him to go out. In so far as possible, avoid ringing them when you open the door for other reasons. Praise your dog if he sniffs or touches the bells. When he pushes or tugs at the bells so they ring, praise him enthusiastically, let him out (or take him out), and when he is finished outside, let him in and give him a treat. Most dogs pick this up within a couple of weeks. Since he is inherently motivated to go outside to relieve himself, your dog will not need continued treats to keep using the bell once he has the idea.

Desensitization and Counterconditioning

These two terms refer to strategies for helping your dog overcome fears (or other problematic emotional reactions like excessive excitement). Once a fearful reaction is established, a dog may be incapable of learning that "nothing bad happens" in connection with the thing that frightens him—the fear he experiences is self-perpetuating.

Desensitization and counterconditioning rely on the idea that your dog's fear is a response to a stimulus, which refers to something that your dog perceives. Thunder is a stimulus that provokes fear in some dogs, for example. The stimulus may be strong, such as loud thunder right overhead, or weak, such as a recording of thunder played at low volume. There is a threshold level of stimulus above which the dog is overwhelmed with self-fulfilling fear, and below which he is capable of learning and adapting.

The idea of desensitization is to expose the dog to the stimulus at a low level, so that he is not reacting strongly and has the chance to experience the stimulus without the fear. As he experiences the stimulus unassociated with anything unpleasant, his tolerance increases, and the threshold at which he strongly reacts increases as well. He can be exposed to increasing intensity of stimulus, pushing his threshold higher and higher until he can tolerate any level he is likely to experience. Care must be taken not to expose a dog to a stimulus for too long, or to progress so fast that he becomes frightened, as that will increase his sensitivity and undo his progress. Recordings of thunderstorms are used in this way to help dogs overcome fear of thunder.

Counterconditioning is trying to change a dog's reaction to a stimulus from fear or anxiety to a more pleasant emotion. The offending stimulus is paired with something pleasant. As with desensitization, the stimulus is kept below threshold so the dog is not overwhelmed and can learn. In training retrievers we sometimes need to retrain a gun-shy dog. We begin with a gunshot at a distance from a gun that is not very loud (such as a blank pistol), and have the person who fires the gun throw something for the dog to retrieve. The dog loves to retrieve and, having previously been taught to retrieve at this distance, soon learns to look in the direction of a distant gunshot in anticipation of a throw. Once this pleasant association is established, we switch to a louder gun (a shotgun) and begin moving the gunner closer to the dog.

As long as we don't rush the process, we can take a dog whose reaction to gunfire is overwhelming and retrain him to respond by looking for an opportunity to retrieve.

Dogs may have fears for different reasons, including past trauma or lack of socialization, i.e. insufficient exposure to a variety of experiences prior to four months of age. Counterconditioning works well in a lot of cases. My husband trained a promising young Labrador named Cricket who could not concentrate at competitions because she was afraid of large men. He developed the strategy of going around to all of the large men ahead of time, asking their help and giving them dog bis-

Counterconditioning as used for a gun-shy dog. The sound of a gunshot is associated with the opportunity to retrieve.

cuits. Then he got Cricket out and walked her up to each one in turn. After a few weekends in which all the large men she met fed her biscuits, Cricket relaxed—and started to do well in field trials. Edible treats are useful in most counterconditioning setups. Choose something your dog especially likes.

Sometimes a dog is so afraid of strangers, or some kind of strangers such as large men or children, that he cannot get close enough for a stranger to give him treats without experiencing intense fear. You can still work to establish more pleasant associations by giving treats yourself. Arrange to have an appropriate person appear at a distance, give treats to the dog continuously as long as he or she is in view, and then stop when the person retreats or disappears again.

As with the gun-shy dog, you can gradually work closer and closer to the frightening person, watching your dog to make sure you don't get too close too quickly and overwhelm him.

In most of the training we do, we give a dog rewards for things he does, creating favorable associations with the activity and the choice he made in doing it. In counterconditioning, we arrange for him to associate treats or pleasant experiences with some thing, some stimulus, so that he will learn to be comfortable in its presence.

Correcting the Cause of the Behavior

Sometimes behavior problems are a consequence of something that stresses and distresses the dog. Identifying and solving the underlying problem is the best possible solution. Dogs may bark, for example, because they are isolated, fearful, hungry, or thirsty. Often the best solution for a dog that is outside barking is to bring him inside the house. Dogs are social animals and prolonged isolation is stressful for most of them.

Dogs can act up in a variety of ways because of fearfulness. They might appear stubborn and reluctant to participate in training or other activities, or they might act aggressive. Identifying the cause as fear can be challenging. I remember videotaping a particularly difficult dog and sending the tape to a behaviorist friend for analysis. I had been training dogs professionally for several years, but did not recognize the signs of fear until they were pointed out to me.

Dogs do not learn well in a state of fear. It is easy to imagine that the thing they fear is taking most of their attention, leaving little to spare for lessons. Once fear is recognized, it is necessary to identify the cause of the fear. If it can be eliminated from the dog's environment, great; if not, a combination of desensitization and counterconditioning is likely to help.

A variety of things can go wrong when dogs are left outdoors unsupervised. Other dogs may challenge them or people may tease them. The invisible containment systems featuring a buried wire and a receiver collar worn by the dog create an opportunity for abuse—children and perhaps adults try to tease or trick the dog into approaching the boundary and getting zapped. Teasing can also occur when a dog is confined behind a physical fence, or chained. Experiences that the owner never sees may lead a dog to exhibit fears, aggression, or inappropriate behavior toward people in general, children, or other dogs. If unexplained behavior problems arise, it is important to review whether your dog is safe and secure when he is unsupervised.

Some dogs are destructive in the home. In many cases these dogs merely like to chew and don't discriminate well between acceptable and unacceptable chew toys. These dogs can be confined in a safe area with approved chew toys for a reasonable length of time. Sometimes, however, destructiveness is a symptom of separation anxiety. Confinement can be extremely distressing to a dog with separation anxiety. It is not always easy for owners to know the cause of destructive behavior. If your dog is of the "Velcro" type, staying by your side all of the time, or if he appears to react emotionally to your putting on your coat and getting your car keys, or if he does damage specifically around the door, or breaks out of a dog crate, he may have separation anxiety.

Full-fledged treatment of separation anxiety is beyond the scope of this book, but easy-to-follow programs are available.* If you think your dog has separation anxiety, please do something about it. He will still love you, and you will spare him a lot of misery.

The Scoop on Punishment

Punishment can have the effect of discouraging unwanted behavior, but the overwhelming majority of punishments attempted by dog owners are ineffective—they are harsh treatments to no good end. Some dogs have little tolerance for harshness and will respond by becoming fearful or aggressive. Others may appear to "take it" well, but lose the trust in their owners they might otherwise have had.

Punishment is commonly misunderstood and misapplied. The reason many problems seem intractable is that the only thing people try is punishment, and it is either inappropriate to the situation or incorrectly used. Armed with an understanding

*An excellent reference is *I'll be Home Soon: How to Prevent and Treat Separation Anxiety*, by Patricia McConnell, Ph.D., McConnell Publishing, Ltd.

of what punishment can and cannot do, you will have a basis for understanding why so many of today's trainers recommend using little or no punishment. If you choose to use punishment in rare cases, you will know the basic "rules" to do so effectively.

There are many reasons punishment is ineffective. One of the most important is the framework in which dog owners understand it. People tend to think that dogs know what they are "supposed" to do, but sometimes choose not to. A punishment, so the thinking goes, will show the dog that the owner is serious, so that he'll shape up and behave. More likely, if a dog is not doing what the owner wants, he does not understand either (1) that the given action is even expected or (2) that the owner will follow through. Owners often expect things that are far beyond their dogs' understanding. Remember that dogs do not generalize as readily as we do, and having learned some command in one setting, are not necessarily prepared to do it when the details are different. Punishment will not improve a dog's understanding.

Second, owners may not realize that timing is a factor. If a punishment occurs much later than the infraction, such as when you come home and find your dog has raided the garbage, your dog will not connect the punishment with his behavior earlier in the day. Even if the delay is just a little, your dog may have obtained a reward that will motivate him to repeat the behavior, regardless of punishment.

A third reason is that frequently what is really needed is for the dog to do some other thing, but punishment gives him no information about that. Punishment, when it works, inhibits behavior. It doesn't encourage behavior.

Fourth, punishment, like medicine, has side effects even when it works. Common side effects are fear and avoidance of the person administering the punishment, the place where the punishment occurred, or other details of the situation. A dog may associate the punishment with the wrong action— perhaps something you have worked hard to teach, but he is now afraid to do. Punishment can lead to poor response to training, as a dog apprehensive about what his owner might do has difficulty learning. Aggression toward a feared person is also possible.

When is punishment effective? First, punishment is effective if it works. If it works, you will see major improvement within the first one or two applications. If the problem continues after three applications, punishment is ineffective. Since it gains you nothing and is almost certainly harmful, it is best abandoned.

A number of requirements must normally be met in order for punishment* to be effective:

Timing: Effective punishment occurs as soon as possible after the initiation of unwanted behavior. If it interrupts the behavior before it can get under way, so much the better.

---

*I am indebted to Daniel F. Tortora, Ph.D. for his explanation of the rules for effective punishment in *Help! This Animal is Driving Me Crazy: Solutions to Your Dog's Behavior Problems,* Putnam Pub Group, 1978.

Degree: Punishment must be forceful enough the first time, or you risk training your dog to endure more and more. It's hard to get right, as you don't want to hurt your dog any more than "necessary," and if he is overwhelmed and traumatized he will develop other problems.

Rarity: Dogs can quickly get used to punishment, rendering it ineffective. By solving as many problems as possible without it, you can keep punishment in reserve for those times it is uniquely effective. Unless you are ingenious at making punishments appear to come from the environment and not you, your dog will associate frequent punishments with you, affecting your relationship.

Fitness: The more a punishment resembles a natural consequence of a dog's actions, the more effective it tends to be. In the "Manners" section of this book I describe a punishment I use on dogs that jump up. I look distressed and back away. I know it's effective because most dogs don't jump on me a second time. I think that it is a good example of fitness. Jumping is a social overture, and my response is social rejection.

Levelheaded Application: Punishment must be applied coolly and carefully in relation to the undesired behavior.

If you are too late and the unwanted action has been completed (or worse, happened some time ago), if you punish your dog frequently, or if the punishment is not clearly related to the dog's action, let it go. Punishment will do no good, only harm, and you are better off without it. If you are inclined to punish your dog because you are angry, stressed, indignant, or even afraid of the dog, don't. You will achieve a better outcome by not responding at all.

Before trying to use punishment to address a behavior problem, consider whether you can come up with a punishment that is well-timed, fitted to the infraction, and the right degree of severity. Can you apply it in a levelheaded manner? Will it be rare, or have you attempted other punishments recently? After the punishment, was there a change in your dog's behavior? Was it the change you wanted? Remember, if punishment works, it will take at most two applications. Please do not keep repeating a punishment that does not get results.

Aggression

Canine aggression is an area of considerable misunderstanding. Frequently people find it unpredictable, and assume it is "unprovoked." My belief is that aggression occurs in a context that makes sense to the dog. Aggression can be dangerous, and it is beyond the scope of this book to purport to tell you how to solve problems of aggression. Many of them are solvable, however. If your dog is acting aggressive, I strongly recommend consulting a behaviorist with experience in aggression. He or she can identify the cause of your dog's aggression, give you an idea what it will take to get it under control, and help you develop a plan. The following information is not intended to take the place of expert help, but to show that aggression is not a great mystery, and that solutions exist for many aggression issues, alarming as they can be.

No one is obliged, however, to keep a dog they believe to be dangerous or a liability. This section is provided for the owner who wants to know how to find information before making a decision, as well as for those who are interested to know a little about the subject.

What is aggression? An obvious expression of aggression is a dog bite. Behaviorists tell us that the general purpose of aggression is to "increase social distance" (think of Yosemite Sam saying, "back off"). This is an important function for a social species, and aggression is considered part of the normal repertoire of behavior in both dogs and humans. A good deal of aggression is "ritualized," consisting mainly of warnings, reducing the need to resort to damaging bites.

Dogs have a sequence of actions they may go through to try to get the message across without having to resort to biting. They "orient," or look in the direction of the offender, freeze, growl, snarl, snap, and finally bite. Any of these steps may be skipped by the dog or overlooked by the observer; don't make the mistake of thinking a dog won't bite because you didn't hear him growl! Bites vary in severity, from milder bites that appear to try to convey a message "will you stop that now?" to damaging, even fatal, bites.

Dogs are extremely quick and have fine control over their

mouths. It is probably a mistake to think "he tried to bite me but I was too quick for him." More likely, the dog did exactly what he intended to do, whether he did not make contact (a snap), barely bit with his front teeth, or landed a more serious bite.

How do you know when you have an aggression problem? If your dog gives any of the signs, the most noticeable of which are growling, snarling, and snapping, he's telling you he doesn't like some situation. If the situation continues his aggression could potentially escalate to biting. If the situation is one that is likely to occur in the future or is unpredictable, for example involving children, who don't always follow our rules, you have a problem.

A common misunderstanding about aggression is that "aggressive" dogs are hostile all of the time. If a dog is relaxed, or sweet and loving, in some situations, owners may conclude that he can't possibly be aggressive, or that the problem is solved. That is a dangerous assumption. Dogs show aggression in response to specific circumstances. Acting appropriately outside of those circumstances, when there is no need for social distance, is no guarantee the dog will be safe when the offending situation reoccurs. If you don't know what triggered your dog's aggression, you don't know when it might happen again.

The first thing to do when a dog shows aggression is to take steps to keep everyone safe. Then try to understand the problem so you can make good decisions about what to do to solve the problem. In the interest of keeping everyone safe, never punish a dog for growling or giving other warning signs of aggression. Two likely effects of punishment are that the dog could develop even more apprehensiveness, i.e. more "need" to act aggressive, and that you might inhibit the warning growl, making it more likely he will bite without warning.

There are a number of typical causes, or situations in which dogs may be aggressive. One is when the dog is ill or in pain. This is probably the easiest possibility to check out and should be your first recourse. A health workup conducted by a vet, with special attention to any issues that might cause pain such as joint problems, may provide a quick answer. If your dog is in pain and the problem is treatable, the aggression can be resolved by correcting the cause.

A second possibility is that the dog is fearful or feels threatened. Fear is not always easy to recognize. An experienced dog person such as a behaviorist, trainer, or vet may be able to help you recognize signs of fear in your dog. Perhaps your dog is not generally fearful but does react strongly to one thing such as tall men, people in hats, or children. Addressing the fear through a program of desensitization and counterconditioning, can make your dog more confident and thus safer. You may also be able to improve his sense of security in general by making sure he has a quiet, safe place where he can retreat, and predictable routines in his life. Dealing with the cause of the problem is the method of choice.

A third type of aggression can occur when the home is permissive and the dog's life lacks structure. Some dogs develop bullying tactics under these conditions. If you would describe yourself as a laissez-faire dog owner, your dog is growling at people or worse, and you feel that he is pushing people around or seems "full of himself," he might be one of these opportunists. Note that lack of structure can also cause a dog to feel insecure, easily threatened—and more likely to bite. There's no contradiction between being insecure and being a bully, in dogs or in humans.

Confronting a bullying dog physically, as suggested by proponents of "alpha theory," is dangerous as well as ineffective. Consultation with an expert would be worth your while, after a veterinary workup to make sure the aggression doesn't have a physical cause. If the expert confirms that the dog is taking advantage of an unstructured home situation and bullying people to get what he wants, the solution may include a NILIF (Nothing In Life Is Free) program. This involves making comprehensive changes to the dog's life so that he doesn't get anything of value—not food, toys, or even free time—without having to "ask permission" of his owners (by responding appropriately to a command). Opportunities to bully people are prevented while the alternative, seeking privileges through appropriate behavior, is taught.

The approach to dog ownership presented in this book includes many elements of NILIF, and is designed to promote good citizenship and prevent pushy behavior from getting started. If you have a dog that is already bullying people, however, a more detailed and formal program may be needed.

A fourth common pattern of aggression is called "resource

guarding." A "resource" can be anything a dog wants, and wishes to keep to himself. Dogs may be possessive of food, bones, toys, food dropped by others, people, other dogs, or a space occupied by the dog. Possessive guarding of people is often mistaken for protectiveness, although it is more a matter of jealously driving away other dogs and people.

Low-level resource guarding in puppies, such as growling over their food, may be outgrown with maturity and sensible training. But guarding behavior can become worse. Every time a dog "successfully" employs aggression to drive others away from what he wants, he is getting rewarded for that behavior. Escalation can occur, leading to dangerous situations. Children are a particular worry. They don't always follow directions and don't anticipate that a dropped toy or food item might suddenly be claimed, aggressively, by the dog.

Protocols exist for dealing with resource guarding. As with the bullying dog, confrontation and challenge are expected to make things worse. A reference for further information is the book, *Mine,* by Jean Donaldson. A good consultant can customize a plan that works for your household, and provide guidance as you follow it.

Some owners prefer to manage their dogs, physically keeping them away from potentially dangerous situations. The problem with that approach is that life is full of unforeseen circumstances that can converge in ways we don't anticipate. By all means, take steps to keep everyone safe, but address the behavior, too.

Aggression can develop through unintended reinforcement (reward), like other problem behavior. Owners may unwittingly encourage "protective" behavior, or reward may occur accidentally. A good consultant will be able to identify the reward and help you put a stop to it, as well as applying multiple techniques to change the behavior.

There are other causes of aggression, some of which lend themselves to behavioral interventions, others of which are more difficult. The purpose of this discussion is to make you aware that aggression is not a black box. A great deal is known about canine aggression, and many cases are solvable if owners are willing to commit their time, the cost of an expert consultation, and, most likely, changes in household routines.

Summary

Most dog behavior problems can be changed or prevented. The key, in many cases, is to get beyond the popular reactions of punishment and "alpha wolf" techniques, and apply some insight into the forces that influence dogs' behavior. This may require some consideration and even changes in household routine, whereas on the surface punishment seems quick and easy to apply. When you recognize, however, that punishment usually doesn't work, instead leading owners to get locked into a perpetual cycle of misbehavior and punishment accompanied by anger and suspicion of the dog, to say nothing of the new problems the dog may develop as a result of punishment, the effort required to do it right seems well-placed.

Yes, unwanted behavior really can be controlled. Dogs are social animals after all; they have social skills, and the ability to learn to be good citizens when we communicate in terms they understand. Try to resist feeling that your dog is invested in his misbehavior, that he "wants" to defy you. He is just repeating the behavior that seemed to make sense when he learned it. My favorite analogy for understanding learning and behavior is that of water cutting a channel. Where the water flows the most, the channel will become the deepest, until all the water naturally flows that way. By guiding a dog into acceptable behavior and preventing unwanted behavior, we cut a channel, i.e. establish a habit, which will endure.

I have tried to provide you with the tools professional trainers use to solve behavior problems. Professional trainers have one more asset—confidence born of experience. You can solve behavior problems with these methods if you believe you can. Trust your dog to learn and trust yourself as a trainer.

LADDIE

Laddie is a Golden retriever, with a strong pedigree of titled working retrievers. At the age of six months, Laddie was on his way to being euthanized for aggression. His family had returned him to his breeder because he had growled at the children, and snapped at their father, when they approached his favorite toys. Back at his breeder's house, Laddie had snatched a tissue from the trash to play keep-away with, according to his breeder, a "look" in his eyes. Laddie's breeder, seeing this as insubordination, had "alpha-rolled" Laddie, grabbing him and forcing him onto his back on the floor. Laddie struggled but his breeder persisted. After some time she finally succeeded in pinning the dog, getting her hand bitten badly enough to draw blood in the process.

The breeder, now frightened of the dog, confined him to a crate with only short walks outside to relieve himself. Shocked at being bitten by a mere puppy, she suspected that the responsible course of action was to have Laddie put to sleep. She consulted other breeders and trainers of her acquaintance for their opinions.

Her friends' opinions were damning. Laddie was not aggressive all of the time, but occasionally would get that "look" in his eyes. This led the breeder's friends to label Laddie a "Jekyll and Hyde dog," unpredictable and therefore dangerous. The

Laddie.

breeder's fear was taken as evidence that Laddie could not be trusted. He had to be "wired wrong." Most of the feedback the breeder received consisted of endorsing her fears and encouraging her to follow through with what needed to be done.

When I heard Laddie's story I thought there was a lot of room for doubt. I believe a dog is entitled to defend himself, and Laddie could well have perceived being grabbed and forced down on his back as an unprovoked assault. Contrary to the opinion of the breeder and her friends, I have found Golden retrievers to be willing to stand up for themselves with their teeth. Considering the damage a dog is capable of doing, I thought the evidence was that Laddie was very restrained in trying to ask his breeder to please stop. Furthermore, I am not intimidated by low-level resource guarding, which is common in Chesapeake Bay Retrievers, with which I have experience.

I told the breeder these things, and found my arm twisted to take the dog. She thought I could train him and sell him to a hunting or competitive home, possibly one where he could be kept in a kennel and be no danger to anyone.

I don't really remember why I agreed to take Laddie, but the following Sunday I drove to the Raleigh-Durham airport to pick him up. I do remember being worried that I was buying heartache: that if Laddie had to be put to death, it would now be my responsibility. I knew that before that decision was reached, I would have feelings for the dog. I did already, just having heard his story.

Most of the time, dogs come into Air Cargo. Air Cargo is really convenient. A big strong guy will lift a dog in his crate, right into the back of my covered pickup. At Raleigh on Sunday evening, however, Air Cargo is closed. The airline told me I'd have to pick the dog up at the baggage claim. The baggage claim is a long walk from the parking garage. There were baggage carts for rent, but I would have had to come all of the way back in to get my deposit back. It was late, I was tired, and I had a long drive to make. I decided that even though the dog now in my possession might be dangerous, I'm enough of a dog handler to get him back to the parking garage under control. I was soon to be reminded that I understand dogs better than I do people.

Reaching into a small space occupied by a dog is one of the

situations where people get bitten, but I did it. I reached in, put a collar and leash on the dog, and led him out. He seemed normal enough at first glance. I attached a second leash to the dog crate and dragged it behind me. I kept a close eye on the dog's behavior. I wasn't thinking about human behavior.

Evidently Golden retrievers are people magnets. Even though Laddie, as a field bred Golden, is small, orange and not fluffy, a crowd materialized somehow in that empty airport and descended on us. Laddie responded to all of the people with a wagging tail and a sparkling demeanor. Not bad considering that he'd been taken from his home, alpha rolled, spent a week in a crate cared for by people who were afraid of him, and just come off a long multi-legged flight. As we walked down the long stairs, crate bumping behind, a chivalrous type dismissed my assertions that I was fine and didn't need help, and hoisted the dog crate high in the air over Laddie's head. Laddie looked up and wagged his tail.

I messed up badly by failing to anticipate that people would gather around Laddie, thus exposing them to a potentially dangerous dog. By the time I got to my truck I knew that whatever issues Laddie might have, he was as secure and confident as they come. I was optimistic about his future, and glad I stuck my neck out to save his life.

I drove Laddie home, put him in the kennel, and began working with him. The first thing I wanted him to do was an informal retrieve, or "play retrieve." Laddie wouldn't retrieve. His previous family had worked with a trainer getting him to trade objects for treats, so when he did pick anything up, he would spit it out again. It appeared, though, that he'd never chased anything. He had no idea of tracking something with his eyes and going after it. I tried throwing different objects, and found that Laddie would sometimes pick up a short piece of white PVC pipe if I threw it a few feet. Most of the time, though, he wouldn't pick it up.

During the time I was trying to get Laddie to retrieve, I hand fed him, getting him to sit in different positions in order to earn handfuls of food. This is one strategy that's recommended for resource guarders. I threw the piece of PVC for him twice every day, and left him alone apart from that, in hopes he would decide chasing the PVC pipe was the most fun he could have. He wasn't much interested, but I kept on. There is a saying that "blood will tell," and it would be surprising if a dog with a pedigree like Laddie's didn't have strong retrieving potential waiting to be awakened.

After three weeks of effort Laddie would consistently retrieve the PVC pipe when I threw it six feet. After that it was easy to get him to go a little farther with each throw, and switch to a vinyl retrieving dummy, which I can throw much farther. I took a risk and tossed a dead bird for him, on the floor inside the kennel. I suspected, given Laddie's breeding, that he would find the bird a highly desirable object. I didn't know if he might guard it. Laddie grabbed the bird and headed out into the night. I caught up with him in the driveway, thanks to the long line he was dragging. As I reached for the bird, a curious cat approached from Laddie's other side. Laddie gave a snarly bark in the direction of the cat as I took the bird. It is interesting that although I was taking the bird from him, Laddie directed his aggression toward the cat.

That is the only instance of aggression I have seen from Laddie in almost three years. Once I got him retrieving, his enthusiasm grew rapidly until he became one of the most motivated retrievers I have trained. Laddie is smart, talented, and has an outstanding attitude toward training. Within a few months he was an accomplished retriever, taking direction through obstacles at distances of 300 yards and more. Retrieving, of course, is all about bringing objects and giving them to the human handler—a good example of a behavior that's incompatible

Laddie retrieving.

with resource guarding. Dogs that learn to love retrieving are intensely motivated to give objects up. That's the way they get another throw.

When my husband and I were invited to demonstrate our retrievers at a community fund-raiser, we took Laddie. After running a couple of more advanced dogs on difficult retrieves, we let the little kids in the audience take turns working with Laddie. He was gentle, but animated, and charmed everyone. We had only one minor problem, which was he kept bringing everything to me at first, but as the kids threw for him again and again, he got the idea.

I also entered Laddie in a "best trick" contest. He didn't know any tricks, but he's a good sport with a sense of fun. I held out a retrieving dummy, stuck out my leg, and told him "fetch." He jumped over my leg and grabbed the dummy in mid-air. A lot of people admired his style, but we lost to a piano-playing Dachshund, who probably had spent more time learning her routine.

I am convinced that Laddie has one of the soundest temperaments I have seen in a dog. It doesn't hurt that his original family did a careful and thorough job of socializing him. So what went wrong? Why was he on death row when I learned about him?

I have talked to other trainers and behaviorists and learned that resource guarding is common in the retriever breeds. Perhaps the desire to seek something, find it, and then carry it around is linked to possessiveness. I've read some case studies and it seems that sometimes intelligent, high-drive dogs can turn into real terrors in a pet home, pushing people around and using aggression to do it. My tentative explanation is that Laddie's problem was that he needed a job. He was bred to do a job, and he's intelligent and hard-working.

In addition, although his former family took Laddie to puppy classes and did many things right, they never taught him to retrieve. Retrieving would probably have motivated

I love this dog.

Laddie to bring things and give them to people, instead of jealously guarding them.

I am a great admirer of working dogs, but Laddie's story has taught me they're not for everyone. I think his tale also illustrates that oft-repeated opinions can be wrong, and that a dog whose problems seem insurmountable can sometimes turn completely around if the key is found.

I changed Laddie's name. He was originally called Lucky (I have another Lucky). I consider myself the lucky one, because I am privileged to own this dog.

INDEX

ABOUT THE AUTHOR

A former college chemistry professor, Amy Dahl has trained dogs and their owners full-time since 1997. While Amy has trained dogs to obedience and hunting test titles, most of her work is with family pets and hunting buddies. She believes the key to good behavior is giving owners the tools to motivate and communicate with their dogs. Amy writes a regular column in *Just Labs Magazine,* and her training articles have appeared in other publications in the US and abroad.